10 STEPS TO

Successful
Time Management

Let's face it: Most people spend their days in chaotic, fast-paced, time- and resource-strained organizations. Finding time for just one more project, assignment, or even learning opportunity—no matter how career enhancing or useful—is difficult to imagine. The *10 Steps* series is designed for today's busy professional who needs advice and guidance on a wide array of topics ranging from project management to people management, from business strategy to decision making and time management, from leading effective meetings to researching and creating a compelling presentation. Each book in this ASTD series promises to take its readers on a journey to solid understanding, with practical application the ultimate destination. This is truly a just-tell-me-what-to-do-now series. You will find action-driven language teamed with examples, worksheets, case studies, and tools to help you quickly implement the right steps and chart a path to your own success. The *10 Steps* series will appeal to a broad business audience from middle managers to upper-level management. Workplace learning and human resource professionals along with other professionals seeking to improve their value proposition in their organizations will find these books a great resource.

10 STEPS TO

Successful Time Management

Cyndi Maxey, CSP

Kevin E. O'Connor, CSP

ASTD PRESS

Alexandria, Virginia

ASTD Press is an internationally renowned source of insightful and practical information on workplace learning and performance topics, including training basics, evaluation and return on investment, instructional systems development, e-learning, leadership, and career development. Visit us at www.astd.org/astdpress.

Ordering information: Books published by ASTD Press can be purchased by visiting the ASTD website at store.astd.org or by calling 800.628.2783 or 703.683.8100.

Library of Congress Control Number: 2009935478
ISBN-10: 1-56286-718-0
ISBN-13: 978-1-56286-718-8

ASTD Press Editorial Staff:
Director: Adam Chesler
Manager, ASTD Press: Jacqueline Edlund-Braun
Project Manager, Content Acquisition: Justin Brusino
Senior Associate Editor: Tora Estep
Associate Editor: Victoria DeVaux
Editorial Assistant: Stephanie Castellano

Editorial, Design, and Production: Abella Publishing Services, LLC
Cover Design: Ana Ilieva Foreman

Printed by Versa Press Inc., East Peoria, IL, www.versapress.com

CONTENTS

PREFACE

We save minutes with techniques.
We save moments with strategies.
We save memories with a mindset.

Our goal as consultants is not to save you time. Rather, it is to save your life—the life you want to live while everything else is getting in your way. Our goal for you in reading this book is not that you will become the master of time but that it will not master you. Our goal for this book is to help you figure out what is most important so you can use your time wisely and productively.

To accomplish these goals, we use what we like to call "an uncommon approach to the common sense of life today," inspired by our favorite teachers and mentors: Viennese psychiatrist Alfred Adler, Chicago psychiatrist Rudolf Dreikurs, and High Point University president Nido Qubein. We have also asked expert colleagues in the field of human development and other learning development professionals to provide their best time tips for trainers and people developers. You'll find their practical and unique ideas throughout the book, along with the best ideas from classic time scholars. It is our intent that the masters will be your teachers, as they have been for us.

If you prefer more of an "over-the-shoulder" view of what we as coaches learn from our clients' challenges with time, you will enjoy the Coach's Corner throughout the book. These are real questions and answers about time and life management that we've encountered. Perhaps you'll see one of your own among them. Here is an example:

Coach's Corner

Q: My to-do list is never-ending. Each day, my tasks—no matter how much I do—are replaced within 24 hours by more. Should my to-do list follow me to the grave?

A: It probably will. Like time poorly used, the list is just a list and ours to use, ignore, or misuse. Here is an idea. Consider using your to-do list as a project blueprint. That way, instead of checking off boxes, you can work from a plan in the same way a building contractor constructs a home.

Group your activities into errands, work, family (and alone) time, study, and so on. Then put each activity into one of those bigger groups. Of course, the details will change from day to day, but your beam, your focus, the "home" you are constructing will remain the same. For some, this grouping helps maintain focus and reduces anxiety.

Another approach is from Qubein. Rather than a to-do list, also have a "to be" list. What do you want most in life? What needs to change? What is your bucket list of things to do before you die (or really start living)? What is your legacy? What do you want it to be?

Finally, the key to time well used will always be organization. Use a daily 3 x 5 card to quickly take notes of situations that occur to you. Later, put the notes in your organizer. A helpful online tool that is also a free application file (app) available for smartphones is www.rememberthemilk.com. Another tool can be found at www.daytimer.com, which is a well-established time management company that produces many useful items both electronic and in print to keep us all at our best. Find one that is simple and easy-to-use and actually works for you. This is a personal decision. Any system works as long as you work it.

The key to the to-do list is organizing toward a goal, not simply checking items off a list each day. While one supports a life well intended and well lived, the other simply shows a calendar with an "X" drawn through each day as if you live in a cell. In the end, what do you want your legacy to be?

As you read this book, we wish you a great adventure—one in which you can live the life you want within the time you have. This book is not meant to be a book of mere techniques and tactics, though you will find plenty. It is not meant solely to save you time, though most certainly you will. Rather, it is a book about what is most important in your life.

And it's about time we all thought differently about that!

Although the 10 steps in the following pages will help you master the complications and the joys of the 168 hours you have every week, we can summarize this entire book for you right now: self-regulation. Bad things happen in anyone's life, including major misfortunes and even occasional disasters, but the fact is that the key to surviving these times is a deep understanding of one's inner authority, inner power, and choice making. Even when faced with a child's (or boss's) temper tantrum, one can take heart with Dr. Dreikurs' famous advice for parents: "Take your sail out of their (children's) wind."

POINTER

The great French Marshall Lyautey once asked his gardener to plant a tree. The gardener objected that the tree was slow growing and would not reach maturity for 100 years. The Marshall replied, "In that case, there is no time to lose; plant it this afternoon!"
—*John F. Kennedy*
(1917–1963)

In life, how often do you fall prey to the easy victim mentality of "poor little old me?" When you feel overwhelmed, ambushed, besieged, busy, overwrought, rushed, and stressed, the victim mentality is an easy and seductive mindset to adopt. But successful, happy people enjoy something their less happy counterparts do not; they control the parts of their lives that they can. The famous Alcoholics Anonymous movement advocates control in all but the first of its 12 steps, which states that the alcoholic must admit he or she is "powerless" over the effects of alcohol. Each ensuing step constructs the result of following step one—a life plan based on self-power, self-regulation, self-control, and self-responsibility.

How Do You "Really" Spend Your Time?

In the same way that some dieters lose weight simply by keeping a record of what they eat, meticulously recording exactly what they eat, you can do the same with time.

As you begin this book you might find it helpful to keep a very accurate record of how you spend your time. Attorneys do this daily to bill their clients, and they do it in 15-minute segments, looking back and recording how they spent the last quarter hour and for whom.

So...pick some major categories of your life: work, family, children, leisure, TV, friends, and so forth. Keep meticulous records of these categories for one week. Then analyze if that is how you want to spend your time. On week two, notice what is changing, better, different.

As simple as this may sound, you may find what many others have found: when you pay attention you become aware and when you are aware you can change things.

Our culture, however, is less enthusiastic about self-regulation. Consider the last time you heard someone blame, bemoan, or judge rather than take responsibility for his or her own actions. How often have you witnessed road rage? How often did you hear about someone who "deserved" special treatment, different and apart from the others? When Kevin's children attended Montessori School, the teacher warned parents that responsibility was to be taught and practiced daily. "If your child forgets his or her lunch, you as the parent can bring it to school if you wish, but we won't give it to your child." Rather, the teacher continued, "We will ask the class to look into their lunches and offer one item to help their classmate." (Most children only forgot once, because every offering from the other lunches was usually the least desirable item!)

If it is to be, it is up to me. This may be common sense, but in our culture, it is easy wisdom to forget.

May you use the next 168 hours in the way you want.

Cyndi Maxey, CSP
Kevin O'Connor, CSP

What You'll Find in This Book

This book is really only about one thing: changing the way you look at time to harness your energy. We often see time as the enemy, as an outside force, as a pressure. We'd like you to look at time differently, and in the pages that follow we hope to help you change your mindset about time!

Step 1: Forget the Myth—Being Busy Isn't Being Productive— Your mindset is what really counts in time management. Some think "busy" is good, some think it is bad, and others are too busy to think about it. Control the way you think about time and your-self, and you will be far ahead of the clock that races after you.

Step 2: Manage Your Energy; Manage Your Life—Although all of us can certainly save minutes and moments with techniques and strategies, what is essential is that we manage our energy and our focus. What you spend time on in the beginning will help you make the most of your time.

Step 3: Be Useful and Stick to the Purpose—Have you ever won-dered why you do what you do? Ever been caught in a spiral of things you have to do? Ever wondered what it all really added up to? Worse, have you found that you are focused on perfection each and every time? Purpose and usefulness will help a lot!

Step 4: Maintain Clarity and Move Forward—Saving time may be a bit of a myth when it comes to knowing what is most important. Many find just how important things are when the tough times come—sickness, loss of a job, financial issues. Knowing and doing what is important is . . . important!

Step 5: Manage to Your Advantage—Identifying your priorities is the key to making the best use of your time. Learn to ask the right questions first.

Step 6: Pay Attention to Your Key Contacts—Knowing who your most important contacts are and focusing attention on them is vital to your success. Learn effective ways to communicate and work with your main contacts.

Step 7: Connect and Get the Most From Your Time—Connection is far different than communication: yet we work with words all day long, emailing, texting, and talking. How many people truly "connect"?

Step 8: Understand the Forces That Affect Your Use of Time and Energy—Instead of managing time, stay focused on energy and engagement.

Step 9: Focus on What Is Significant—Selection of your life is a critical element to satisfaction. While some toil for retirement, others know that life is now.

Step 10: Make Time Your Friend—Time is inside of you and is under your control. Be wary of placing too much burden on yourself by the measure of others. In this final chapter, we help you contribute to your organization without being dominated by it.

ACKNOWLEDGMENTS

For our editor, Mark Morrow, who inspired us to think more closely about time and energy. For our mentor, Nido Qubein, who always helps us think differently about that which is so easy to take for granted. For the great psychiatrists, Alfred Adler and Rudolf Drei-kurs, whose groundbreaking work in the field of human relations is felt more than 100 years later. For Julie Kaiser, whose expertise made the words come together. For all the dedicated friends and professionals who allowed us to quote their best tips for successful time management. And for our best teachers—our clients—who let us know every day how precious that day is in terms of how they use their time, unleash their energy, and make a difference to all who come into contact with them—including us!

DEDICATION

For all my Chicagoland Chapter ASTD friends and colleagues, who since 1982 have taught me the value of time dedicated to caring professional, volunteer, and family relationships. Thank you especially to Janet Frazer, Darlene Dunmore, Barry Lyerly, Ed Gordon, and Stan Piskorski, who trusted me when I was new to the field, and in memory of Larry Kennedy, who introduced me to ASTD.

—Cyndi Maxey

For my colleague, mentor, and friend, Bob Gilbert.
Like many of us, Bob is often on time and often not on time; always however giving the gift of focused time, attention, and energy to others with obvious and enduring respect. This is the mark of service, growth, and leadership.

—Kevin E. O'Connor

Forget the Myth—Being Busy Isn't Being Productive

OVERVIEW

Avoid "activity addiction"

Master the "meet, met, meat" principle

Get more out of your time through self-reflection

"How are you?"

Do you find when you ask a friend or colleague how she is, she frequently responds, "Busy, really busy!" Sometimes it is hard to tell if she is exasperated, distracted, or proud. Although our lives can certainly be demanding, fast paced, and hurried, "busy" has become a nondescriptive word similar to the often related nondescriptive answer, "fine." Both "fine" and "busy" cover up the truth of what is really going on. This step's goal is to illuminate the truths and dispel the myths of being busy while making sure that the person in charge of your time and life is you.

"I'm Really Busy"

A friend or colleague's pained yet often proud expression, "I'm really busy!" leaves us wondering how to respond. If we probe with, "And how's that working for you?" we set ourselves up for

Some people blame others for their problems or bad moods. There's just one problem with this. Others get the blame; they keep the problem. It is when we take full responsibility for the creation of every single moment and every single thing in our lives that we are truly free.

—*Jim Accetta, MA, MCC*
Inspirational Speaker, Author, Personal Life Coach

a barrage of cities traveled, deadlines, family events, and a panoply of time-consuming issues that amount to "busy-ness"—occupied time that is neither free nor necessarily meaningful.

Do you want your physician to be busy when he or she examines you? How about if your boss was distracted during your performance appraisal? Do you want his complete attention, or is it OK if he "multitasks" in your presence? Or how about when you really want to talk with your parents and they are "busy!"?

Too often, a busy person is an overwhelmed one, on a treadmill, expending energy, and going nowhere. Do you really admire all of this "busy-ness"? Do you really admire busy people? Should you admire them or pity them? Are you, too, among the "really" busy ones? Could it be you have become addicted to activity regardless of the outcome? Did you ever wonder if all the emails, voicemails, and endless to-do lists are necessary?

You've heard many colleagues brag about the 50, 75, 100, 200, or more emails they receive each day. Is this productivity or merely the appearance of productivity? A common example is when you strive to clean out your email inbox—not just to read the emails but to get some subconscious relief. While doing so, you've made your company no money, you've advanced your agenda not one iota further, and you've not really connected with anyone or anything.

Identify Who's in Charge of Your Life

In the early 1900s, the great Viennese psychiatrist Alfred Adler speculated that all we do is purposeful. We behave the way we do because it suits our purpose—sometimes a purpose that we are unaware of at the time. For example, children sometimes misbehave to annoy us, but their actions are not so much to annoy as to catch and demand our attention. Sometimes adolescents don't complete their homework, not so much out of rebellion or boredom but rather out of fear of failure. "If I don't try, I can't fail!" says their inner thinking. When you are busy and when you multitask, could it be that you are really just procrastinating?

> POINTER
>
> Regret and fear are the twin thieves that rob us of today.
>
> —*Unknown*

We recently surveyed three groups of high-level managers with a simple question: "What percentage of your meetings are total wastes of your time?" The majority responded that 40–50 percent of their meetings were a complete waste of time; one responded 20 percent but then told us he was new and only had to attend two meetings per month (lucky him!). These managers were probably not the only ones who thought the meetings were a waste of time. And yet, who speaks up? Who breaks the pattern? And why don't they?

How about you? What has your life been like lately? Who is in charge of it?

10 Important Reminders and Other Life Realities

Here are some reminders and realities to dispel the myth of busyness and to double-check that the person in charge of your life is you.

- ◆ **It is easier to be busy than to be productive.** When is the last time a friend or colleague answered, "Productive!" to your "How are you?" question? Yet it is well known that the words you use affect your thoughts as much as your thoughts affect your words. Try describing your day as "pleasantly productive," "a blend of creative and practical stuff," "best one this week," "nice," "beautiful," or anything other than "busy." See what kind of response you get. You can begin with a story or an example when you find that the description of your day is becoming boring and routine. For example, when asked how his day was going recently, one of our clients responded, "Organized chaos!" Then he went on with a concise story telling us about the organized part and the part that was chaos. He ended by saying, "And I like it that way."

◆ **Email is addictive.** How much time did you spend staring at your email today? Worse, how many colleagues did you automatically "copy" with everything in your inbox? How satisfied do you feel about just getting through your emails when instead you should be asking the ultimate question: "What did reading my emails accomplish for me today?" You can get through many emails and not make a dime for the cause, not increase membership by a single person, and not really move the enterprise forward one bit. It's not because you have poor intentions, rather it is because you are using email the wrong way. Like a student "studying" for a test by staring at a book, you are thinking wrongly from the start. What if you saw emails as a connection or intersection and not as an inbox? Would you treat some of the mail differently? What if your email was your town square? Thinking this way, your job is not to get through with the task, but rather to get through to the person. You save time when you connect with email rather than merely respond to it.

- **Returning voicemails is an adult form of "tag, you're it."** Have you played that game? Or do you give every voicemail a headline up front, along with a concise, thorough answer to what you want next and the best way to get back to you? Voicemail only works when you prepare for it in advance and use it to move forward, not to play a game of tag. Like email, everyone listening to a voicemail has two questions he or she wants answered before deciding to cooperate with you:
  - What is this?
  - What does it have to do with me?

  Answer those questions early and often, and you will certainly be a "connector" . . . and you will have time on your hands.

- **The cell phone is convenient, but it can undermine your ability to focus.** Depending on the audience and those around you, using your cell phone can be unnecessary, unusually rude, or, in some cases, completely unacceptable. Imagine the times you have used your cell phone when the call could have waited. Were you surrounded by others who are on their cell phones and completely out of touch with the here and now? Was it in a restaurant, in an airline terminal, in heavy traffic, in a meeting, at a school conference, or a child's little league game perhaps? Have you made calls from a public washroom? Are any of us so important that we need to be that accessible? And must the rest of the world listen to us while we think we are that important? Rather, we need to be aware of the need for privacy, the importance of social grace to others, and the influence we have on those who can make or break our careers. They won't tell us how it affects them, but they will make a career decision based on this and more. Make a break from technology at meetings, especially when your boss and the boss's boss are there. Never check your electronic device—never! Save time by being fully present to those in attendance. The perception others have of those who are tech-free (and fully present) is that *they* feel attended to.

◆ **When you are late, regardless of the reason, you are probably kidding yourself as to the real reason.** People learn to trust punctual people. Are you late because what you were supposed to be on time for was simply not important to you? When you're late, the reason has to do with your way of choosing priorities, understanding your feelings toward the person or the appointment, and knowing yourself. Traffic is rarely the reason. You are the reason. What if you made a determination today to never be late, even to be there early to use that time to engage, discuss, or plant ideas? What if you saw the brief time before a meeting begins as your networking time or your influencing time?

◆ **The leader's job is never to *look busy* but rather to be inquisitive, interested, calmly competent, and respected.** If you have a busy boss, does that really feel like a good thing? Many of the best bosses use the "meet, met, meat" principle. They know that to accomplish anything of substance, they have to *meet* the other person, gain his or her trust, and engage in a relationship. They know that having this meeting will render a memory for the other person that they have *met*. This also burns an image in the mind of the leader that you are important, unforgettable. Finally, leaders remind us of the *meat* that you can share together. This is the substance of your meeting, the thing you can do together now that you have met. What would your chance and arranged meetings be like if you implemented the meet, met, meat method? Adopted in this way, there will never be another meeting, wedding, funeral, or party that is a waste for you . . . as you meet, met, and threw some meat to others.

◆ **If you can't connect with me within 24 hours, you are way too busy . . . or think you are.** There is great satisfaction in being able to respond within 24 hours. This does not mean you have to meet every deadline within 24 hours but simply that you have responded and that others know they have connected with you. Telecommunications today allow fast connections; people know that and expect timely responses more than ever before. Just a note that says, "I received your email and am working on it. I'll get back to you with details soon" will suffice.

◆ **Your quiet time today at work and at home will probably be your most productive time . . . and truthfully, few of us use it enough.** What if you scheduled some right now? Try something other than a "close the door and work" session. How about a "close the door and reflect" session? Creativity experts have long taught the importance of the incubation step for eliciting and evaluating ideas. Early morning reflection or a walk at the end of the day provides quiet time for busy professionals. But what if you go one step further? Instead of doing something, what if instead you planned, thought through, and decided?

◆ **Don't kid yourself, your family, or even your stockholders.** You are neither irreplaceable, nor are you so important that life won't go on without you. We are surrounded with meaning and with seeming meaninglessness: People die too soon; lives are cut short, incomplete. It is as if whatever we are doing now is extremely important and yet in an instant it can be altered, changed, even over. Awareness is the key that reminds us we are both important and replaceable. Are you truly aware of this tightrope of meaning and meaninglessness that you walk? You are busy, and yet if a loved one is taken to the emergency room, do you really have to think about it? Or worse: Is what you are doing now so very important to you that it could be seen as falsely urgent, addictive, and misguided by those you work with?

Here is one simple time-saving technique: Monitor your smile and your enjoyment of the moment. Those who believe themselves to be superhuman waste an enormous amount of resources focusing on the *what* rather than the *who*.

◆ **The busy part of you is not as important as the productive part.** What are your three or four (maximum) goals in your life? If you have to achieve anything with your life, what is it to be? Alan Lakein, author of the classic book *How to Get Control of Your Time and Your Life*, recommends you always ask the "golden question": What is the best use of my time right now? Try asking yourself that question often during each day. The answers will be surprising.

Listen to Your Own Rhythms

Physicians have long suggested that we listen to our own natural circadian rhythm. When are you at your best? Some of us truly are morning people. Others really do wake up after dark. Rather than trying to fit things and people into a schedule, how can you build your activities around your own natural best? One of our colleagues snacks throughout the day and then eats lunch after 3:00 p.m. because he says lunch just makes him sleepy.

Gary Richards, an OhioHealth executive, uses the term *activity addiction* when he wants to remind himself of what is important versus what might be just personally satisfying. Just like addictions to food, drugs, thrill seeking, gambling, and alcohol, we can become addicted to meaningless activities when we use them to excess. This addictive quality makes us turn inward rather than outward toward others and toward productivity.

High Point University president Nido Qubein thinks about time differently. Instead of thinking minutes and hours, he manages time in terms of five-minute units or 15-minute segments. If someone wants an hour of his time, he thinks in terms of 12 units or

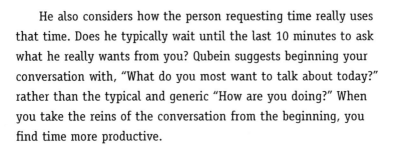

four segments. This allows him to better determine what the worth of that invested time really is and helps him think less generically about an hour as one of 24 and more as a precious parcel of time right now.

He also considers how the person requesting time really uses that time. Does he typically wait until the last 10 minutes to ask what he really wants from you? Qubein suggests beginning your conversation with, "What do you most want to talk about today?" rather than the typical and generic "How are you doing?" When you take the reins of the conversation from the beginning, you find time more productive.

Four Plans of Productivity

Consider the diagram in Figure 1.1. You'll see a broader version of this later in the book. For now, notice the Four Plans associated with your productivity. The circles represent the dynamic forces that you engage in every day. These are the forces that shape your day and your time.

Circle #1 is about your history; your organization's structure; your family's past; and the important legacy that every person, event, and organization has that shapes its present and its future.

Circle #2 is your personal experience of life, how you view it, understand it, and make sense of it for yourself. Although you may encounter history and the traditions of others, you have your own perspective. When a friend returns from Europe with stories of the Eiffel Tower, the Tower of London, or even the special coffee shop in Leuven, his or her eyes and words are full of history. When you ask, "How was that for you?" you get an even deeper insight into the trip—that person's personal experience.

Circle #3 focuses on your professional and personal skills—the toolbox that you carry each and every day. Some of you are the masters of the interpersonal, others of the financial, and still

FIGURE 1.1

Four Plans of Productivity

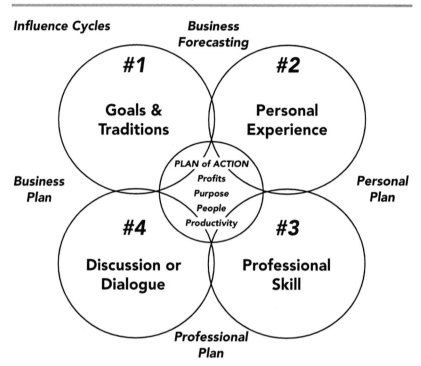

others of how to swing a hammer or operate a construction crane. These skills help you navigate the world. The better you are at these skills, the more effective you are day to day.

Circle #4 is your ability to enter into the world of the other—to engage and cooperate, negotiate and achieve consensus, and educate and develop. These interpersonal interactions and discussions are the sum total of the other three circles but are distinct unto themselves because so much of your life is wrapped around others. The middle circle represents the fruit of your labors. These five circles are dynamic, constantly changing, moving, and interacting. The closer you allow the circles to overlap, the larger your middle circle is—your influence with and over time.

Build Your Plan

Each circle combined with one other can prompt you to make the first step in your time journey—the plan. The plan is at the heart of a self-regulated life. When you understand the dynamic forces in your life that lead you to productivity and purpose, you can also go about the important business of creating and following the plan—and this puts you in charge of your own world. Have a personal business plan in addition to the real business plan. It will be a critical guide for you—a time saver, a life saver, and a career saver, too.

> **Business Plan:** Your personal business plan will primarily be the combination of your knowledge of the business (goals and traditions) and your interactions with others (discussion and dialogue). Every new employee, and even veteran employees after a major change, must engage in understanding the system, the organization, and the people. Without knowledge of the business and your interactions with others, as well as a studied approach, your time will be chaotic as will your business plan.
>
> **Business Forecasting Plan:** What is coming down the road that you need to know will be a combination of the organizational culture, its "system-ness," and your personal experience in the profession and on the job. Here is where you will find your own personal wisdom. This is why experienced and engaged veterans of the company can provide you with valuable understanding. Retired politicians earn big incomes becoming advisors because they can finally say what they want rather than say what they think others want them to say. Comedian Jay Leno remarked on *The Tonight Show* during the writers' strike, when few celebrities would cross the picket line to pitch their latest movies, "Now, I can finally tell everyone what I really think of these movies!"
>
> **Personal Plan:** Your personal plan will be an outgrowth of your personal experiences and your professional skills.

This is your value to the organization and to your team. We often advise clients interviewing for a job that they construct a 90-day plan—what are they going to do when they get the job (not if they get it)? Every employer wants to know more of what you will do, not as much of what you have done.

Professional Plan: This plan, too, is personal, but comprises your skills and the skills of others in communication with one another. The others may not always want to communicate. They may want to compete, demand, and bully—all the more reasons to have a plan based on skill.

The point is that successful people have a plan that saves them time, money, and effort, and perhaps influences their careers. This book is about making that plan. Worksheet 1.1, at the end of this chapter, can help you build your plan.

Here's What to Remember

What keeps you going? What probably should? What do you really want? This is the question asked at the beginning of this book. Instead of seeking tips and techniques to save time, you will save your life when you reflect on yourself, your actions, and especially your attitudes.

Coach's Corner

Q: I find many meetings are not necessary. They drag on and on and on. If it is my meeting, I can easily speed things up. What if my boss is running the meeting?

A: Consider becoming even more engaged in these meetings. Lead, even if it isn't your meeting. Be alive, awake, and connected, and make motions that inspire action. Hop up and use the flip chart, ask open-ended questions, and summarize often. When it comes time to schedule the next meeting, make some alternative motions. If nothing else, this approach will keep you awake and alert, which is often impressive to bosses and to their bosses.

WORKSHEET 1.1

Getting ready to save some time: A personal initial assessment

1. Time saving is like dieting, we do better when we have data. A good dieter knows exactly what he or she ate today and last week because of a food diary. Consider keeping a time/energy diary. For at least one week, note what you did and when, how much time it took, and who else was involved.

2. Think of the 10 most important people in your personal life and the 25 most important people in your business life and list their names. Over the next month, put a check next to their name each day you personally meet with them, speak to them, or interact with them.

3. Look at your schedule and your checkbook. Where you spend your time and your money is a keen insight into your future direction in life.

4. Ask others who know you for three words that describe you in relation to time and energy. Don't argue with them! Simply accept each word and the explanation and move on to the next person. Notice any patterns—especially the surprising ones.

5. And finally, how do you feel about your use of time? Where do you applaud yourself? Where do you feel you are falling short? Who loses besides you?

Mindset Questions for This Chapter:

1. What are you noticing about your thinking about time just since the last chapter?

2. What have you done recently, even in a small way, that made more sense to you time-wise?

3. What else are you aware of that is happening in your life because of questions 1 and 2?

NOTES

_____

_____

_____

_____

_____

_____

_____

_____

_____

_____

_____

_____

_____

_____

_____

_____

_____

_____

_____

_____

Manage Your Energy;
Manage Your Life

OVERVIEW

- Harness energy rather than time
- Mirror the traits of accomplishers
- Choose a system that works for you

Although each of us has only 168 hours per week to do with as we choose, how often do we really take advantage of the word *choose* when we engage in those waking and sleeping hours? The schedules of work and play, the requests and the demands of others, even the need to refresh and relax take time from us. When we focus only on time management, rather than look at a broader perspective, we may save minutes; however, a different focus—energy management—can save us a life.

Manage Your Emotions and Energy

Psychologist Alfred Adler thought that emotions were the gasoline in our tank (*The New York Times*, 2009). Emotions do not drive and direct us, but they fuel us—as long as we keep them in our tank doing what they are supposed to do. Allow the fuel to leak out, however, and we experience an explosion.

The first part of managing your energy has to do with knowing what your fuel is and where it belongs, as well as where the

Time is the coin of your life. It is the only coin you have, and only you can determine how it will be spent. Be careful lest you let other people spend it for you.

—*Carl Sandburg*
(1878–1967)

driver's seat is and who belongs there. How often do your tasks mix with your emotional states? Daily situations such as deadlines, directives, emergencies, and even "Quick, let's have some fun!" events all contribute to the emotional leakage that is part of your day. Each comes with a demand and an emotional response. And the emotional response can get you into trouble: a meltdown at a meeting, a distraction while driving, a quickly written angry email sent, even a lapse in judgement and too little time to prepare for a training session—all of these situations are more than events, they are emotional situations, too.

In these difficult circumstances, emotions can be seen as unnecessary and unwanted eruptions. What if you saw them as forces of energy that you can understand, harness, and use instead? One way to do this is to make sure you use them to help focus on your work rather than distract you from it.

Write It Down

Many time management experts suggest writing down what you want and need to do as soon as it enters your awareness. Author and consultant David Allen (*Getting Things Done*), for example, postulates that the brain wants to work, and if you give it something to work on, it will work and work and work until it finds a place. Emotions want to emote! And as you know, they will emote, emote, and emote until you do something about it. Like a two-year-old child who wants her mom's attention, emotions are relentless. A simple task such as remembering to go to the dry cleaners will take up valuable brain space unless you move it out of the brain space and put it down on paper. This creates more brain room available for other important endeavors such as "must find ice cream!"

One of my favorite ways to manage time and energy is to apply one of the principles I taught during a Kaizen event. Kaizen means continuous improvement, and one of the strategies we taught was to streamline and organize work processes to minimize steps to complete a project. If you organize your activities, you will be amazed how you can save time and energy. In the event, we saved our press operators so many steps in their job, by reorganizing the order in which they did their tasks, that they actually felt much less tired at the end of the day.

—Linda Polinski, Director of Staff Development,
Lutheran Life Services

Writing down tasks and lists helps you organize, but what if you also attached a note to symbolize your emotion about it? One or two or more exclamation marks, a red check mark, or a bold font are all ways to express emotion, and perhaps also the urgency, you attach to the task. If everything on your list looks just like the rest, then there is no expression of the emotion. Write it down and make it express what it really means to you.

How you move it out of your head and onto the list is not as important as finding the right process for transferring the idea or information. Years ago, information often went on a 3 × 5 card carried in a pocket. Handy, easy to carry, and providing a written record of the day, this simple technique is still used by many executives around the world. Using 3 × 5 cards, which are small enough to make details or projects seem manageable, eliminates multiple sheets or sticky notes and requires no batteries. They are also easily filed away in a card file for safekeeping.

The to-do list is another eternally popular method of giving yourself brain space. Once written on the list, a task, no matter how large or small, seems more real—more do-able. And if you're like most list makers, you've got a favorite pad, pen, and place for that list. You check and change it habitually, which allows for easy use. What if in addition to writing the "what" of the task down, you also wrote the "when"? Not simply the due date, the "when" can be a reminder of when you are going to work on it. This can then be put in your calendar as an appointment with yourself. Use your calendar for these appointments with yourself and see what flies off your to-do list.

Certainly many electronic tools are available to capture all of this: iPhone applications, talk-to-text pens, and other gadgets. Whatever you choose, make it simple, quick, and efficient to move it out of your head and onto something else. Make room in your brain. Once you have it on paper or in another form, you can rely on this external link to your brain rather than your memory, no matter how good your memory is (or used to be). Your brain can be used for better things than your daily lists, like how you want to live your life.

Once you have your lists out of your brain, you have more thinking options, which is the whole point of time and energy management. You don't want clutter on your desk or in your mind, at least not the kind of clutter that complicates or distracts.

One advantage of keeping cards or lists is that it allows you to take a look at how you might be cluttering up your life after a week or so. What is your week composed of? Is this what you really want? A wise person once said, "If you want to know what is important in your life, you need only check your calendar and your checkbook." Our time and money are usually indicative of our priorities, and yet we are not always fully conscious of either over time, at least not until the credit card statement comes in the mail. Written records have a way of encouraging accountability.

Become Aware of Emotions

Time constrains us; our energy is most likely boundless. Time is not under our control, but it can be within our mastery. *New York Times* film critic, A.O. Scott, commented that Julia Child

Timebits

When we say, "You can't manage time, you can only manage your energy," we speak of an energy composed of three essential ingredients:

STEP 2

- ◆ **Your mindset.** This includes your awareness and your approach. Although some people have a sunny attitude and a pleasant disposition, others have storm clouds that follow them. Still others seem to be in a bit of a fog, turned inward, seemingly not connected to who or what is going on around them. Mindset energy can be our pre-programmed self or an intentional mindset—how we decide to approach awareness and how we allow our awareness to help our approach.

- ◆ **Your preparation.** This involves your ability to step back first, to thoughtfully consider, to calm your anxiety or panic, and to develop a plan, if only one that works for the next moment. Research is just now emerging about how survivors of plane crashes, home fires, and public panics are the ones who keep their head about them in the very first moments. They make deliberative plans for what to do in the next instant. Knowing where the fire exits are located is one thing; knowing what you would do to reach them may mark you as the survivor. We all know where the exits are on an airplane; knowing exactly how many rows you are from the exits while seated on the plane can determine how accurate you are in reaching them.

- ◆ **Your courage.** This is your willingness to take the next right step, even knowing it may not be quite right yet. Courage helps your energy deal with the constraints of time. Real courage has an element of risk, not chance. Chance is a fleeting opportunity fraught with danger and excitement. It is not just a roll of the dice at the craps table; chance is not recognizing the rules of the table, the odds, or the possibilities that create a losing streak. Winners don't really control the dice; they control the table. Winners also know when to walk away. Risk, however, is more deliberative, thoughtful, and aware. The individual who risks does so with emotion and thought, with knowledge and anticipation, with adrenalin and calm purpose.

was a cook, not a chef. "The book is *Mastering the Art of French Cooking*—not 'How to' or 'Made Easy' or 'For Dummies,' but 'Mastering the Art.' In other words, cooking that omelet is part of a demanding, exalted discipline not to be entered into frivolously or casually. But at the same time: You can do it. It is a matter of technique, of skill, of practice." The book, he continues, "fundamentally altered the way a basic human activity was perceived and pursued."

And so it is with our time conundrum. If we think we have control, we are perceiving and pursuing wrongly, even wrong headedly. Instead, it is ourselves we need to be aware of, to control, and to use. We are our best tools, not our electronics.

At a recent professional conference, conversation buzzed around technology, websites, and social this and social that. An electronic flu seemingly infected every hallway conversation, every seminar, every after-dinner drink. We were all contaminated.

As a result, we behaved very differently at this conference. As if in a third- or fourth-world country, I watched the food truck unload while hungry recipients grabbed all they could as fast as they could with no apparent regard for why, what, where, when, or how.

When the dust cleared, I hoped each of us would be nourished by the frenzy, but I doubted it. The only ones I felt any hope for were those who asked why, what, where, when, and how thoughtfully, carefully, and intelligently. I didn't meet too many people like this, but when I did, they stood out in their calmness, their selectiveness, and their obvious choice making.

I wondered as I encountered the calm ones if they knew something, some secret something that the rest of us were ignoring. Beyond this conference, how did they handle the constraints of time? Did questions, not more resources, really inform better? Could it be that selective adoption of technology and even selectively listening to "the buzz" allowed them time, gave them time, perhaps fostered their use of time in a more practical way?

Some words help us handle the constraints of time more than other words. Consider these juxtapositions:

- intentional not reactive
- thoughtful not automatic
- preparation not immediate
- self not technology
- trust not suspicion
- courage not fear
- risk not chance
- outcome not activity
- useful not perfect
- early not rushed
- calm not anxious
- inner not outer
- no refers to another person, relationship emphasis
- joy.

Dr. Chin is a physician leader who constantly extols the virtue of having fun at work. Recently, he made one additional, essential point: Fun at work is for the ultimate purpose of finding joy.

Joy is enduring; fun is transitional and transactional. Our fun feeds our joy, it sets us up for joy, but it is not joy itself. Shopping for some can be fun, but like many quasi-addictions, it can lack a transformation, a future, and a hope for more. By understanding and repositioning our end goal, we can perceive and pursue it differently.

In a recent survey of 706 adults, 75 percent said they were either not looking forward to their family reunion at all (23 percent) or only somewhat/not too much (52 percent). When we know a family reunion is not about the food or the conversation or the shared memories of the past, but rather about the experience, then we may use our time differently, perhaps in a better way, with an enduring outcome—perhaps even one of joy.

Dr. Chin went on to say, "Trust reduces the cost of every transaction." Without trust, there is no real business to our lives, only suspicion, self-concern, and secrecy. With trust in others and mostly in ourselves, we function more freely. Like the difference between fun and joy, trust also has its own outcome—comfort.

To reach that comfort, however, the cost of every transaction cannot only be measured financially. Comfort has to do with our integrity, our purpose, and our reputation. Although the phrase, "trust but verify" carries weight in today's geopolitical world, in our world, trust allows us to trust and collaborate, cooperate, and connect.

What does all of this have to do with time? It may be that joy, trust, and courage—the three endpoints of our activities—are what this whole time management enterprise is all about. The intermingling of the three is to use our time well rather than to scrounge for every last morsel of the minute before us.

Time is the wind; we control the sails and the rudder. Time is the ocean; we control our strokes and kicks and our scuba gear. Time can be fire; we know how many rows to the exit. Time is time; we control our equipment and mostly ourselves.

Make Long-Term Plans

What if you reversed the process and planned how you want to spend your week or month in advance? What if you took that week or month and looked at it in the same way you plan a vacation: "I want to go here on this date, stay at this hotel, do these activities, stay an allotted time, and know when I'm coming home." Often, however, you plunge into a week knowing the barebones schedule of commuting, working, lunching, and commuting. Everything else is squished in between. Within the confines of work, you have deadlines, meetings, and emergencies. You even have to make room for other people's emergencies, which they would like to become yours.

Why not decide in advance what kind of a week you will have, what it will mean, who it is for, what you want most to accomplish, and what you also will not do? You'll accomplish this best through reflection, which is not something many of us are too good at because we "don't have the time for it." When you make the time for it regularly, however, and do so intentionally, almost reverently, you may find your week is a very different reality than if you just plunge in. For some, Sunday evening is a good time to prepare for the week ahead; for some, it may be the Friday afternoon wrap-up; and others find that first flight out a great time to reflect, prepare, organize, and chart the week and the energy ahead.

Imagine what happens to your emotions when you prevent leakage by making room in your brain, reflecting and planning your week in terms of what you will and will not do. This can take less than a fraction of an hour and yet deliver you a lifetime and a lifeline. A physician executive coach we know counsels doctors in mid-life career choices that they recognize and understand their preferences. She uses the Myers-Briggs Type Indicator, one of the most researched psychological assessments in the world. Her point is that when you do things you can do but do not prefer to do, you deplete your energy. Sometimes unknowingly, you find life becoming more and more difficult, boring, and unsatisfying. You may or may not need an assessment to know this, but when you find your energy sapped along the way, it could be that you are neglecting your preferences.

Timebits

"I felt like I was the expert in the room," a client confided one day after a particularly successful meeting. He was exactly right. When you run a meeting or are the featured person at a meeting (even for a short, 10-minute update), regard yourself as the expert and the room as yours. This is what your audience, your colleagues, and your boss want, though they will often not tell you that.

Bring Your Preferences Front and Center

Consider the following ways to bring your preferences to the forefront:

◆ **Reflect:** What are the parts of the week that you love, the engagements you prefer, the priorities, the people, and the life you experience when you are living your week well?

◆ **Write:** Keep a diary of what you liked this week. Dieters often keep a diary of what they eat to control their behavior. What if you kept a list of those events this week that really made you feel alive, important, useful, and on track? Imagine how useful that information would be the next time you search for a response to the standard question, "What's new?" (It would certainly be a better response than "Not much, you?")

◆ **Rest your voice:** Soul singer Aretha Franklin, in the middle of her third decade of performing with her powerful voice, said it took just that long, 30 plus years, for her to realize the secret to keeping her voice. After her concerts, she simply does not talk for 20 minutes. Giving the voice a rest helps keep her vocal cords in shape. She doesn't take them for granted. How about you? Consider doing the same with your schedule. Take a short break and consult your week's plan. Are you on schedule, doing mostly what you prefer, keeping perspective, and staying on track?

Mirror the Traits of Those Who Get It Done

Upon careful study, it appears that people who seem to accomplish a lot have these things in common:

◆ **Goals:** They know the destination they are headed for, the next job they want, and what will make them feel successful as well as be successful.

◆ **Targets:** Different than goals, they know who they want to target their efforts for and toward. They are aware of who is who and why these people are important. From Mother Teresa to Donald Trump, these people know who is important to their success.

◆ **Vision:** This is a clear image of what, for them, is a vital component of their energy. The restaurateur knows the ambiance he wants at his eatery, the masseuse knows what

Timebits

Never neglect the time-saving interpersonal skill of the paraphrase. Restating concisely in your own words what the other has told you will save an enormous amount of time by avoiding misunderstandings, arguments, and resentments. Recent research has shown that up to 50 percent of the time, patients exiting a meeting with their physician did not feel they told their doctor all of their symptoms. Why? The doctor interrupted them and didn't listen. In fact, the average amount of time a doctor listens before interrupting is 20 seconds. (One doctor in the research interrupted after three seconds.)

The resulting errors and misdiagnoses (not to mention bad feelings and resentments) are mind-boggling. Understanding thoroughly first saves time in and out of the doctor's office.

atmosphere she wants for her clients, and the university president can see in his mind's eye the new building years before ground is broken. These visions are clear, compelling, and crisp.

◆ **Abiding picture:** Regardless of what comes their way, these accomplishers keep the picture in front of them. This is why they always seem to be taking one step forward after another. Despite disappointments, the abiding picture keeps the movement forward.

◆ **An overriding outcome:** For these people, the outcome is so important that literally nothing stands in their way. They want it, they know it, they can see it, and they can feel it. Our restaurateur can even taste it!

◆ **A belief in self:** Imagine the self-confidence these folks have (or at least appear to have). Many an accomplisher is not always confident, but they act, as Viennese psychiatrist Alfred Adler (*Practice and Theory of Individual Psychology*) suggested, "as if" they have it. When you act "as if," very interesting things happen.

◆ **Abundant understanding of the value of failure:** Speak to any successful person and ask him or her one simple question: "Have you ever failed?" You will get an earful of swings, misses, and outs. Many of us fail because we fear failure. Accomplishers use failure.

♦ **A clear mission for success:** Regardless of the failures and speed bumps along the way, accomplishers are very clear about what success looks like to them. How else could single mothers work and go to school? How else could the unknown among us come from nowhere and become senators, presidents, and Supreme Court justices? How else could you put three men on top of a bomb full of explosive material and have them gently land on the moon?

These productive people all have something guiding them that began deep within them, and it lingers in their consciousness every day. Their every activity helps them sort, select, and succeed in their choices. For some, this occurs from an early age. An Indian physician half-jokingly said that in his native India, when a child is two years old, the parents present the child with one of two books as a birthday present—an engineering textbook or a medical textbook. He laughed and said, "I am not really joking!" Then he laughed again. He explained how his parents really believed he could pursue any dream he wanted, as long as he had a passion for success. "I fought them for a while; then I realized they were right!" he said with a smile. Another Indian doctor knowingly nodded in agreement. From early in life, our parents help us understand what is important.

Even those who do not have these early experiences are usually driven by something deep inside that is personal and that is personally important to them. Ask anyone about his or her formative years, and you will find a treasure trove of hits and misses, thrills and regrets, role models and cads who taught them more than any school.

So, too, we learn to use failure; the importance of others; and a strong sense of rightness, virtue, responsibility, and valor. All of these values and traits form the core of a person. In a way, the values and traits make them who they are, drive them relentlessly, and fuel them.

The productive ones also seem to be quietly obsessive perfectionists who don't mind momentary, incremental, and normal failure en route to success. They also don't let their perfectionism get in the way of understanding their imperfection. They are savvy to the ways of the world, of others, and of themselves.

Make Better Use of Your Mistakes

How do you handle mistakes; errors; failures; and those people who manipulate, hurt, or work from selfish motives? Do they stop you, delay you, derail you, or freeze your efforts? This is a critical piece of information we must learn from despite our desire to do well all the time. No productive or successful person has made achievements without experiencing failure. Biographies are littered with details about great people making superlative errors, encountering withering criticism, and being steeped in incredible self-doubt. Chicago psychiatrist and author Rudolf Dreikurs (*Social Equality: The Challenge for Today*) recommends having the "courage to be imperfect," which will enable you not to achieve perfection but to be useful. This is what he considered to be a sign of good mental health.

T i m e b i t s

Financial advisor Travis Chaney advises, "I have plenty of electronic and human reminders for myself to stay on track, but I also use pen and paper for lists and reminders. I'm not averse to electronics, but neither am I to paper."

It is not easy, though, to err, especially in a world that prides itself on planning, perfection, process, and productivity. But when we reflect, all of those activities serve a greater purpose. That purpose is more along the lines of Dreikurs' recommendation: to be useful to others so they can connect, learn, and be useful, too.

Our culture is often not kind when mistakes are made. Criticism, blame, and ridicule usually follow. Paparazzi spend their time looking for a celebrity's embarassing moment or mistake; commentators on many sides of important issues are ready at a moment's notice to take the opposing position; and it is easy to be quietly judgmental when differences are noticed.

Choose Your System

Accomplishers use a personal system that helps their brain operate with enough space and without dangerous distraction. Ask successful people about their systems, and they will know immediately what you are talking about. They have a reliable way of going through their world and their workday. They have a routine, a method, a way, and a process that helps them move with ease from one situation to the next. An elementary version of these systems can be found in a variety of stores. Office supply stores sell paper planners with a calendar system; file folders are touted with a file management system; even home supply stores have a system for organizing your closet. These appeal to us because we can envision ourselves as finally complete, successful, and organized.

You want a system, but which one should you choose? The truth is that any system will work if you follow it. The system is a processing station, not a decision-making system. If emotions are the fuel and you are in the driver's seat, the system is your GPS helping to navigate the journey and allowing your brain to think about what to do when you arrive.

POINTER

I prepare a 3 × 5 card (so it fits in my shirt pocket) of what I want to accomplish the next day. This focuses me for my end-of-the-day progress review to see if my day was successful from a goal perspective.

—*Tom Girton, FACMPE,*
Business Manager
Pediatrics Center, Glen
Allen, Virginia

So pick a system and stick with it. The productive ones know it isn't the system that makes the difference, but what the system allows them to do that makes the difference. But what if you have no clue about a system for success? How do you learn from, rather than compare yourself with, those who seem to do so much more? Try simply reflecting on what is important to you. What do you want? How would you like it? This cannot be a dreamy "If I think it, then I will get it" approach. Rather, take a vacation

> **Timebits**
>
> Leadership saves time. Leadership focuses meetings in a way that service alone does not. When you serve, you often defer, wait, hold back, and look to someone else to give you the "go" signal.
>
> When you lead, you sit in the driver's seat. When you know the way, your job is to move from here to there. There should also be a place and a voice for the passengers. Every leader needs to lead someone. Be aware that at any given moment, the follower—the passenger—can lead with contribution, direction, and participation. The driver is not the only leader.

approach. Where would you like to go? Is your budget tight this year? OK, so where would you like to go anyway given your resources? What would you like to have happen there? With whom? You don't have to be rich or famous or even superlatively talented to map out what you want.

And while you are at it, go easy (and easier) on yourself. Overcoming perfectionist tendencies is very difficult. This is almost as difficult as it is for someone who never felt special enough, didn't deserve much, and felt downright ordinary. While the perfectionists overachieve, others are underachievers. There are those who are afraid of success. They look at the target and confidently say, "Yes, I could do that! I don't want to, but I could!" Despite the look of confidence, this is fear talking, and it takes its ruthless toll over the course of a lifetime.

Consider your system. Are you willing to try something new? Hurry on down to the office supply store and buy 100 3 × 5 cards. Implement your 3 × 5 card strategy for the life of the stack, one per day, one extra for your weekly reflection day. Then just watch and notice the difference. Your brain will be free. The rest will be up to you.

Take it from the productive ones—the accomplishers— a system that works for you is crucial.

Coach's Corner

Q: When I am presenting with PowerPoint, I notice I always have about five to 15 slides left as my time runs out. My rehearsal is always on time, but when I'm in front of the audience, something happens. I race through the slides with a slight apology so I can finish them all. Any tips on how I can align my rehearsal time with my presentation time?

A: Rehearsal time does not equal presentation time—ever. Always build in time that allows for the audience and you to interact, something you don't have in rehearsal. If they laugh or if you pause, it all takes time. Bottom line? Cut out some slides.

World travel expert Arthur Frommer recommends that when packing for a vacation, you lay out the clothes you want to take and reduce them by half. Then, with the half remaining, cut that number in half again. Now, you are ready to pack. The same is true with PowerPoint presentations: edit, cut, delete, eliminate, shorten, and focus. You will give the audience what they really came for—you, not your slides. Is it a technical or medical presentation? Put all of your complicated slides in the back as archive slides readily accessible by you or your audience later. There should always be a difference between your presentation slides and your archive slides—only one set will help you connect and communicate.

Next, never rush your ending. Have your final slide built in toward the potential end of the talk. That way you can end on it, and no one will be the wiser. Simply type the number and push "enter." Your PowerPoint will automatically bring up that slide. Fast, smooth, and less distracting than going through slide after slide searching for the right one!

Consider using a flip chart to end your program . . . or not. On your PC or Mac, hit the "B" key and this will black out your PowerPoint screen. You'll now have the attention of everyone in the room. Then, go to the flip chart and put one word on the chart in very large letters. End your talk on that one word.

Or try this instead: Simply walk toward the audience and say something like, "So, there are really three things I want all of us to take away today . . . ."

Know that if you are tempted again to race through those slides, only one thing is happening for the audience—they are checking out. And you have lost even more precious moments that could be lasting moments of influence.

Timebits

My friend and client, Bob, asked for ideas regarding time, how to save it, use it, and not be defeated by it. Here are some answers.

◆ **Decide when to turn you "on" and when to turn you "off."** Nido Quebein, president of High Point University, recommends a different way of looking at time. Think of your time not in minutes but in units. Each unit is five minutes. So if someone asks to have an hour meeting with you or a lunch away from the office, you can say to yourself, "Good Lord, that's 12 units!" instead of "Sure!" The units approach will give you a new perspective on time and mostly how it is being used or abused by others or by you.

◆ **Be very, very selective about meetings you attend and for how long.** There is no reason you need to be at every meeting for the entire meeting. Be selective about your meetings upstairs also. You will be more help to them if you position yourself as their consultant rather than reporting to them, having to be perfect, anxious, anticipatory, and afraid. They are lucky to have you. Let them know what you think and ask the unasked question.

◆ **Keep the team aware of wasted meeting time.** Have them tell you the alternatives, and keep it fresh in their minds that just because we've always done things this way doesn't mean we always have to.

◆ **Ask, coax, implore, and require your team to do more.** There is no reason you should have to edit their work as precisely as you do. They need to do a better job with what they give you. One of my health care clients told me recently, "Teams here are huge . . . as is accountability." Have them deliver to you as a team and then hold them accountable for its quality, its promptness, and its usability.

◆ **Finish early, earlier, on time.** One oncologist I know always leaves the office at 5:00 p.m. He is the most productive doctor in his group, makes the most money, has the highest patient satisfaction scores, and then he goes home every night. He has said he is not smarter than his colleagues. He believes he does three things the others do not. From the beginning of his workday, he is constantly aware of time. Furthermore, he is prepared for every encounter and every patient. He knows what he wants to have happen during his time with them. Finally, when he is with them, he is with them. His focus is intense. Although he sees more patients per day than anyone else in his practice (many who struggle with life-and-death issues), he consistently satisfies his patients. How would you like a doctor who was (a) on time, (b) prepared, and (c) focused entirely on you? Would you count the minutes, or would you count your blessings? He cautioned me that all of this expends effort and energy. Time is constantly on his mind during the workday.

◆ **Focus.** Your weekly email summarizing the week and forecasting the next has been a big hit with the team. Before you send the next one, ruthlessly edit it to see what it looks like in terms of impact, readability, and length.

◆ **Seek even more feedback**—not so much to judge whether you are right or not, but to be absolutely sure the target of your communication got it right. Do this as often as you can with everyone you can. Assume nothing. This will confirm for you that you were heard ("Tell me what you heard me say/what you hear that I wanted/what I need from you and when"). This approach will help them listen better (some listen to you out of and with a great deal of anxiety of their own making), and it will create accountability (no more "I didn't understand").

◆ **Slow down, close your door, look out the window, and really think about outcomes as much as the details of your day.** At your town hall meetings, keep those outcomes in the back of your mind as well as on your lips. Give yourself detail time and outcome time, thinking time and technology time, right-now time and long-range time. Don't do just one of these all day long.

◆ **Obtain a bigger white board that you can move around the floor and write on**—in your office, the break room, the hallway, the elevators, and so on. White boards help you visualize and think through issues. They can also create awareness for others. Even at a meeting, you can stand up and go in the hallway to have a quick meeting with the moveable white board. Not a bad idea for others to see how you think, what you expect, and how decisions are made.

◆ **Begin every meeting—every one of them—by asking, "How's your time?"** When they respond, you then say, "I have 15 minutes, so let's get as much done now as we can and reschedule the rest if needed another time soon." Have Sarah come in and interrupt your meetings at an arranged time, maybe with two minutes to go. When she does, stand up and begin to summarize the meeting, even if it is not finished yet. Recap and give a call to action and accountability. Ask them to summarize and say what they will do and when. Be the "new Bob" here, friendly of course, but firmly rooted with focus.

Here's What to Remember

◆ Make and take the time to ask yourself what you really want.

◆ Find a way to give your brain a break from remembering unimportant things by transferring them to your index cards or other system.

◆ Keep a log of some of your mistakes and then later on, write the good that may have come from that error.

◆ Read about the lives of others during lunch instead of reading your magazines, having your lunches with the same old people, or eating at your desk while you work.

◆ Make a stop-doing list.

◆ Rest your voice.

◆ Interview someone who seems productive and see how he or she matches up with this chapter. (Be sure to ask about his or her formative years.)

◆ Think energy, not time.

◆ Tell no one of your newfound system of thinking and acting. Simply do it privately. Then watch how they react to the new you.

Mindset Questions for This Chapter:

1. What are you noticing about your thinking about time just since the last chapter?

2. What have you done recently, even in a small way, that made more sense to you time-wise?

3. What else are you aware of that is happening in your life because of questions 1 and 2?

WORKSHEET 2.1

Reflect and Sketch

Let's do a checkup. Sketch out the following with only a few words or symbols (or even experiences) and then take some time to sit and reflect, remember, and reconnect with yourself.

What are your goals?

What is your target?

If someone asked for your personal vision, what would you say to him or her?

If you drew your abiding picture, what would it look like?
Go ahead, draw it here!

What outcome do you want more than any other?

What's a recent example of your belief in yourself?

Had a good failure lately? What did you learn about yourself?

What is your real mission, your real definition of success?

Be Useful and Stick to the Purpose

Focus on being useful instead of being perfect

Move away from false ideas and avoid time traps

Use the Competency Model for productive interactions

Consider the perfectionists you know at work and perhaps the perfectionist part of yourself. How many really make an impact, move the enterprise forward, and are seen as movers and shakers in your world? When you honestly admit to your own tendencies to be perfect, how does it feel? Most people respond, "Not that great." So why does doing things perfectly haunt the halls of potential success? If perfection is your goal, you may be starting in the wrong direction, with the wrong premise. You may never see the window opening to the next opportunity.

The psychiatrist Rudolf Dreikurs advanced the concept that to be useful was more important than to be perfect. His most famous speech was titled "The Courage to Be Imperfect," in which he detailed the notion that perfectionists really focus on themselves, while those who deliver useful value focus on others and the world. When you focus on others and the world, Dreikurs maintained, you achieve the ultimate basis for mental health—a concept both he and psychiatrist Alfred Adler called "social interest."

I think the purpose of life is to be useful, to be responsible, to be honorable, to be compassionate. It is, after all, to matter: to count, to stand for something, to have made some difference that you lived at all.

—*Leo C. Rosten*

It may seem odd that focusing on others helps manage your time better. Yet, think of those you know who do it well. John Blumberg, a professional speaker and author of inspirational books *Silent Alarm* and *Good to the Core*, comes to mind. Blumberg has an extensive network that he formed throughout a career in speaking and accounting—a large piece of it due to the loyalty he developed among colleagues who were all affected by the disbanding of a large accounting organization. Rather than letting go of them, he strengthened their network, and now, years later in other jobs, they help each other in many ways.

Use Productivity Leakage to Reflect and Re-engage

It is easy to suffer from productivity leakage and yet barely be aware of it. In today's society, when you feel you are not producing enough, you work harder and faster and seek to do more. In fact, highly productive people (while being highly focused) are not always busy and engaged in work. When they experience productivity leakage, they slow down, reflect, and re-engage with the task differently. Just watch them at work or at home. They betray not a glimmer of panic, though they are very aware of time; not a sense of busy, though they certainly know how to plan their day; not a feeling of resentment, though they have plenty to do. Rather than allowing their emotions or those of others to gain the upper hand, they engage instead in a mindset of self-decision. This decision-making quality allows them to clarify their life's purpose and to consult that purpose early and often as they decide how their days, weeks, and months will go.

Our colleague Cheryl Kuba, gerontologist and author of the book *Navigating the Journey of Aging Parents*, communicates that calm commitment to purpose. Having cared for her own elderly parents, she focuses her time now on helping others care for theirs, through writing, speaking, and consulting—her strengths. Cheryl always has an easy smile, a calm demeanor, and a way of being that unifies with her purpose.

Avoid False Ideas that Waste Time, Money, and Energy

It's easy to get trapped in habits based on false ideas. Catch yourself when you make comments such as these:

- "I can do this myself." Even if you can, you should resist. In your attempt to do it yourself, you save time on the front end but waste even more on the back end. Resist the urge to go forward alone.
- "I'd better hurry." Why? Do you really have to do as much as you think you do even when deadlines loom? Maybe you can just take the next right step and ask for input rather than streaking to the finish line.
- "I have to impress them." Remember, if I'm your boss, your value is in helping me solve the problem, not making me like you. I may like you, but if you can't help me, that is about as far as it will go.
- "Perfect is the goal." Not so. Useful is far more . . . useful!
- "I want them to like me." You may want to be liked, but they will like you much more if you help, facilitate, assist, and make yourself useful.
- "I can show them!" Sure you can. Show them best by helping them feel successful.
- "They'll be sorry." No, they won't. Revenge is never a good strategy for your career. Yes, it feels delicious sometimes, but so do all those wasted calories you take in each day. Think, and then act.

◆ "I'm not up for this, and I don't want to do it." What if you just did it, and then you'll have time to eat.

As you can see, commitment to clear purpose begins with positive thoughts and ideas. Although it's easy to get caught up in old habits and negative mindsets, it's just as easy to reframe them.

> Useful Phrases When You Feel on the Spot
> ◆ Hearing you say that, I . . .
> ◆ I want . . . (I need your help) . . . because . . .
> ◆ I'd like to get some things out in the open about . . .
> ◆ I have different (a slightly different) perspective . . .
> ◆ What I appreciate most about this (you, your perspective) is . . .
> (Adapted from Susan Campbell, *Saying What's Real*; HJ Kramer Books, 2005)

Avoid Time Traps that Muddy a Clear Purpose

In addition to false ideas, time traps can catch the most well-intended time manager. These traps are grounded in how you manage expectations, planning, and goal setting, and how you anticipate conflicts and the unexpected. Here are some to watch:

◆ Romanticized expectations: There can be a tendency for many of us to romanticize, to make grand, and to expand our expectations prior to beginning a project, a party, or a presentation. Although you want your efforts to succeed, you can plant the seeds of poor timing by overestimating your success from the beginning.

◆ Inadequate planning: Live your schedule "one day ahead." Set a planning time each and every day when you think ahead, reconfirm, and connect to your purpose. For example, when you need to bring material—even a mere piece of paper—to a meeting, consider making a folder for it so that all you have to remember is the folder, not what is supposed to be in it. Then you can grab it and go. When you arrive, you will appear organized and ready to begin.

Your colleagues and your family will trust you more when you are on time and ready.

◆ Bad planning: Knowing if your plan is weak (or worse) is often difficult unless you involve others. In much the same way, you cannot predict traffic jams unless you listen to the radio reports. The same is true with planning. Involve others early and often, especially those who are the targets of your plan. When you give them the plan, write "draft" at the top and ask for their input. Do this even in a selling or persuading situation. When you involve them, they can roll up their sleeves and focus on what they want rather than on what you got right. This moves the idea along. In every group, there will be those who will focus on the idea, those who will analyze, and those who will execute. Appeal to all—gather them to the table with your "draft" idea.

◆ Unclear outcomes: Good salespeople always talk about the benefits of the item they're selling. For example, they tell us how clean the clothes will be, not the ins and outs of washing machine mechanics. They help us feel the ride of the new car, not what kind of suspension it has. They want us to know how happy our children will be with the new school, not the budget figures from the last school year.

Similarly, when you work individually or with a group, focus first on the benefits to the receiver, even if you are the only receiver, rather than jumping to the ins and outs of the plan. Focus on the goal and the benefits. This saves you time by avoiding backtracking, going off target, or becoming unclear.

STEP 1

Purpose can be used for good or ill. One might say that dictators, criminals, and bad bosses have purpose, focus, and strong implementation skills. This is true, of course. But purpose without social interest is not purpose at all; it is the work of a discouraged person—a person who wants power, who wants to get even, who thinks winning is all that counts, or who exists to defeat others.

The purpose we are speaking of in this chapter is purpose born of encouragement. Ultimately, each of us has to open our awareness and see just how we are purposeful. Are we moving through life for ourselves or for our contribution?

> Change your mindset without therapy. These thoughts will save you time every time:
> - I'm capable.
> - I'm connected.
> - I'm confident.
> - I'm committed.
> - I'm caring.
> - I can do this . . . and I will.

Zig Ziglar was fond of saying, "You can get anything you want from life if only you will help everyone else to get what he or she wants." The focus can be external, but the drive must come from the internal place.

Use the Competency Model

When you want to work with, develop, or even convince someone or a team, it is easy to waste valuable time by focusing on yourself alone. More than a few of our clients spend enormous amounts of time constructing an argument while unknowingly avoiding even the beginnings of an agreement. Our culture is so saturated with the need to compete, to win, and to convince that we often neglect what good (successful) arguers know very well. First, put yourself in the shoes of the other to understand their position. This allows them to be more open to understanding your position as well. Continuing the argument rarely works; searching for points of agreement often works best.

Figure 3.1, the Competency Model, is a flow chart that describes the mental and interactive time-saving process of competently showing value and helping someone else solve a problem, while perhaps solving your own problem. Without a good understanding of this process, you waste not only minutes and hours but also energy and resources.

The real purpose of a well-timed interaction is to ensure that all you do is purposeful. When it is such, you use the time well with minimal backsliding, greater cooperation from others, and clearer purpose of mind.

This nine-step process is not meant to be a cookie-cutter model. This process is a roadmap to successful interactions that conserve your time and, more important, conserve your energy.

When you first decide to focus your attention on the other (#1), you consider the question, the issue at hand, or the world of the other, rather than yourself. This gives you the time to prepare and saves valuable time by focusing on the target of your attention. Preparing leads to the tentative consultation (#2) when you think about what the interaction with the other person will be like. A version of a dress rehearsal, you are now equipped with a focus (#1) and an understanding of what the interaction will be like (#2). When you do approach the other person, the time will be used to set the stage (#3) so that your interpersonal message is appropriately focused. It does you no good to begin an interaction with a question too focused on what you want without in some way showing appreciation, respect, and gratitude for the other. This is the verbal equivalent of a handshake. In ancient times, the handshake indicated that you had no weapon in your hand, that your intent was peaceful, and that you had no ill will. Today, it is easy to be so intent on what you want, you forget the verbal equivalent of, "I mean no ill will."

FIGURE 3.1

The Competency Model

The Competency Model is a time-saving interpersonal model that allows for communicating value. Value is defined by the other person as "Can you help me solve my problem?" This is the ultimate in working more effectively with others—helping them come to a solution.

1. *Prepare:* Focus on the audience or the other person's message.

2. *Tentative Consultation:* Frame the topic briefly to understand the intent, with questions that teach to the conclusion.

3. *Initiate with Thoughtfulness, Focus, and Thankfulness:* Use your interpersonal and emotional skills early and often.

4. *Consultation with Questioning:* Discuss with mutuality in mind, not arguments to win.

5. *Deliver with Respectful Dialogue:* Link, add, educate, and understand.

6. *Assertive Consulting:* Firm and friendly, slow and steady with options, recommendations, and "going forwards."

7. *Answer with Encouraging Engagement:* Find common ground.

8. *Collaborate with a Consulting Mindset:* Given what you've discussed, what can you do now?

9. *Follow Up with a Targeted Purpose:* Continue to help with a purpose in mind.

You are now ready to engage (#4 and #5). With questions, discussion, and dialogue, you have a better opportunity to educate, lead, consider, and understand. If you enter into this dialogue with an argument rather than a point of view, you are likely to stop the process dead in its tracks. If all you want to do is win, you may achieve that, but many would call this a hollow victory because you have coerced rather than convinced. The old adage that one who is "convinced against one's will is of the same opinion still" is as true today as hundreds of years ago.

When the engagement becomes deeper (#6 and #7), minds often begin to change, opinions lead to consensus, and agreements begin to form. At this point, it is easy to lose focus without liberal doses of encouragement, common ground, and repetition of agreements made. If there are delicate moments in the interaction, this is where they occur the most.

> POINTER
>
> We are not disturbed by things but rather by the view we take of them. When we meet with troubles, become anxious or distressed, let us never blame anything but our opinions about things.
>
> —*Epictetus,*
> *55–135 AD*

Finally (#8 and #9), you reach for more agreement, begin to cement your understanding with one another, and target your purposes together.

Observations to Consider

Look at #3 in Figure 3.1. How many times have colleagues thanked you early in a process? When this happened, how did you feel? What did this do to your emotional fuel level? Be truly thankful. This should never be manipulative. Like the practice of yoga, getting your mind in the right frame is as important as getting your body in the right pose. Thanking the other and finding what you appreciate about the person is an entree that few others can effectively replicate.

Think about #6. When discussions get more contentious, more disagreements flare. When the demands of others become apparent, how often do you find others "firm and friendly"? You can be, and you can be effectively. Never throw gasoline on a fire. Refuse to fire back. Never attempt to win by overpowering. Simply understand that the bark is often worse than the bite and if you wait it out with patience and sincerity, you will have more chances to make your point.

Pick any number in the model and fill in your own understanding of what it means to you for each project you are engaged in. Relate the model to what is in your life now and use it again and again to remind, rekindle, and renew your next right step.

You may even want to keep the Competency Model handy at your next meeting so that when the process begins, your competency will shine through for them and for you.

Here's What to Remember

- Use time rather than be constrained by it. Begin well and in a complete manner.
- Lay out the entire plan, including the time required along the way.
- Be clear about outcomes—yours and theirs—and stick to them.
- Don't complicate (or allow anyone else to). Always go for clarity and elegant simplicity.
- Check in along the way using a "draft" approach with those who are the stakeholders.
- Engage both sides of your brain on projects—think and feel.
- Give yourself an isolation booth. No multitasking allowed!
- Repeat a mental mantra of thoughts that propel you.
- Be aware of the social interest of your purpose.
- Strive for usefulness rather than perfection.

WORKSHEET 3.1

Getting Serious About Usefulness

Our lives can be dominated by our desire for perfection causing us to forget the importance of usefulness. Take this short quiz and rate yourself 1–5 (5 being high, happy, content; 1 being unhappy, frustrated, spinning your wheels).

1. How perfect do things have to be for you?

2. How perfect do the people you live with and work with have to be for you?

3. How conscious are you when you schedule your time?

4. How conscious are you when someone else wants some of your time?

5. How clear are you about outcomes—whether going to the store for food or taking on a task from your boss?

Essay questions:

a. Write an example of a situation when you really had a handle on your time, when you were in charge!

b. What frustrates you most about your own use of time now?

c. Describe a recent situation when you felt the time you spent doing something was useful, even though it may not have been perfect.

Mindset Questions for This Chapter:

1. What are you noticing about your thinking about time just since the last chapter?

2. What have you done recently, even in a small way, that made more sense to you time-wise?

3. What else are you aware of that is happening in your life because of questions 1 and 2?

NOTES

Maintain Clarity and Move Forward

OVERVIEW

Recognize your most
common default
behavior patterns

Gain clarity to stop
stalling

Speak up to save time

Important events often become shuttled to the side while you do things that feel good but are not helpful for you or your organization. How many times have you mindlessly cleared out a loaded inbox on your computer rather than quickly and selectively reviewed those items of importance and value? Executives do this; why not you? How often have you sat in or even arranged meetings that appear of little value without questioning? How often have you remained silent when you needed to be the one to speak up? In each instance, time passes you by along with importance. In your effort to either save time or ignore it, you waste the importance of the moment.

What is your time default—the habit you automatically return to without thinking? Some clean out the email box, surf the web, or clean off the desktop, while others list, plan, re-edit, dream, or even eat. What you do when you don't really want to do

POINTER

Nothing is a waste of time if you use the experience wisely.

—*Auguste Rodin*

(1840–1917)

anything is called your default behavior pattern. Your default pattern is also when you confuse and overwhelm yourself. You do these things when you are not clearly focused.

Think about driving to work in the morning. You arrive at the office and remember little of the trip you take day in and day out. Default patterns are those easy, comforting, and time-consuming activities that provide an illusion of doing, when their real purpose is to distract you from doing what you need to do, are required to do, or could transform you in some important way.

So why do you fall back on these patterns? Default patterns prevent you from being productive in new ways, ways you may be unfamiliar with, or ways that challenge you. In short, a knee-jerk response to change and fear of change lock you into a dangerous present tense instead of allowing you to move courageously into the next future moment. Like a child with a blanket or pacifier, you get comfort from laboring over that email inbox, but cleaning out messages is a never-ending task that doesn't make the company money, move the enterprise forward, or even connect you with the right people.

How do you determine the next right step, the important thing to do, or the essential task? You move to that next step when you clarify. This may seem a simple solution, but recall a recent time when you stalled, hesitated, or distracted yourself from doing what you knew you needed to do. Were you really clear about what to do, who to do it with, and what the right outcome should be?

We recently opened a fortune cookie that read: "Courage is action when the outcome is uncertain." It sounded pithy and wise, and yet upon further examination, we wondered if courage might be the next right step to take toward our self-selected goals. It could involve bravery, but it need not. It could be, and often is, seen as risky, but doesn't have to be. In fact, many courageous decisions, even those made in a split second, are often born of a deliberative process that clarified the situation. Firefighters are viewed as brave, when, in fact, they know precisely what they are doing. With a conviction born of their training and talent, they display courage loaded with self-confidence, preparation, and clarity.

When You're Stalled, Clarify

The next time you stall, wait, or go limp, be sure to clarify. You can do this in many ways. Here are a few favorites:

- Talk to yourself and trust others. You need others you can trust, and even others who see things differently than you do. Say aloud your options and ask for a non-judgmental response.
- Write. Journaling is an age-old way of clarifying the most complicated issue. Write and write some more, edit ruthlessly, and see what persists.
- Think. What would happen if this or that scenario played out? What is the best, worst, and most likely thing that might happen? What do you most want to happen?
- Experiment. Take a small step to build your confidence with just a piece of the puzzle. One incremental step is often all you need to escape a box you might be trapped in.
- Plan. Make a road map from here to there and notice what happens to your thinking (and to your defaults).
- Draw. Without words, on a large piece of paper, draw out your dream for this initiative. Link it to others, and see what emerges. The artist does not always know the outcome.
- Question. Quakers have a concept called a "clearance committee." When faced with an important decision, they ask a group of trusted associates to simply ask questions. No advice or judgments are given, just a series of questions until clarity occurs.
- Take a step. It does not have to be the perfect or even the correct step—it need only be a step.

My favorite time management tip is to use Outlook's Tasks list. It's easy to get overwhelmed by a large project. So, instead of being consumed by it, I break it down into smaller tasks, making sure to create a due date for each one in Outlook. I start with the final due date and work my way backward so I can manage my time and the project in smaller chunks—and Outlook reminds me automatically when something is due so I don't have to keep notes myself.

—Teresa Peavy
Government Relations Coordinator, Academy of General Dentistry

Important moves toward important goals require that you select, prioritize, and choose what to do when, with whom, and for what purpose. Although this is not always an easy task, it is especially important for organizations. A friend who worked on a three-page policy change for more than eight months in a complex corporate environment found that obtaining the CEO's signature required one final meeting with him. Armed with statistics, scenarios, and signatures, he prepared for the meeting with the CEO. At the meeting, the CEO asked one question: "Did all of my direct reports sign off on this?" When "yes" was the answer, the signature flowed. When you have to make your important move, consider these tips:

- Do your homework. Know the lay of the land, know the data, know the procedures, and know both your stuff and theirs.
- Know who is who. As in the previous scenario, while one might assume the CEO was the power, the real power was with his direct reports.
- Determine where the influence is. When physician groups attempt to persuade physicians to join them, they know the physician's spouse is also a key decision maker in the process. They ignore the spouse at their own peril.
- Think like the other person. This is one of the most neglected of all skills and yet the most central.
- Make the signature easy to give. When push comes to shove, go easy—real easy.

What often looks like an easy decision made by others is rarely so. One actor remarked that his "overnight" success happened because of the 20 years that came before that night. How about you?

Is your expertise a fluke, a gift, or luck? Or is it more likely the result of your hard-won experience?

The same is true of our day-to-day decisions. Resist the idea that you have to know the right thing to do rather than trusting your know-how to reach that decision. This is often done with and through the help of others. You waste time if you do this all yourself. Smart managers and leaders involve others early and often.

Gain Control of the Process With the Three *As* of Intended Success

We refer to Figure 4.1 as the Three *As* of Intended Success. Of the three, which one do you think is more important? At first, when we taught this model, we were fairly certain that affability was the most critical component. That worked fine until a student made an awfully good case for ability. Then another student made a case for availability. One said all three were important. You can imagine the discussion. Yes, they are all important—in various degrees and in various situations.

One problem we notice in our consulting and in our classes is that too many people habitually choose one over the other rather than see them as a toolbox from which to choose the best one for the job. When it comes to time, remember that your concern is not so much the clock as it is your response, your usefulness, and your outcome with the clock ticking in the background.

You will gain more control over what is important when you control the process to get to your goal. This

POINTER

I enjoy having quick informal check-ins with my team every morning. This is a great way for my team and me to make sure we are on track with all of our projects/deliverables and daily goings-on to make sure there is not a duplication of efforts. I also use this time as a general temperature check of my team.

—*Andy Katzman*
HR Manager, Time Out Chicago *magazine*

FIGURE 4.1

The Three As of Intended Success

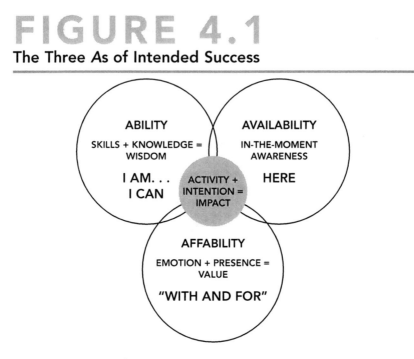

requires you to speak up at meetings, speak up when you disagree, speak to a solution, and speak your mind by incorporating their ideas into your words. Be able, available, and affable. These three As are about awareness, skill, and impact. Use them to bring yourself to awareness and to use the skill we will consider next.

Speak Up to Save Time Later

Making sure that you are actively involved in meetings (even if you are an introvert) will save enormous amounts of time, energy, and effort for yourself and others. Without your input, imagine the delays, the resentments, and the discouragement you may be causing in yourself and in others.

Speaking up is not always easy, but it will help you and others to maintain clarity and focus. If you are unsure what to say, resist the temptation to stay silent. Instead, act interested, paraphrase, or ask an affirming question that helps others talk more. Use simple language such as

- What I like about what you said was . . . .
- It sounds like you are suggesting that we could benefit from . . . .
- Just to make sure I got that right, may I restate your position?
- Thank you.
- I like the basis of your idea. What is your best guess about how much time (money, personnel, resources, and so on) is involved?

The important secret (and in some of today's organizations, it is a well-kept secret!) is to affirm the person and the idea, even if you ultimately disagree. To begin with disagreement or an attack only puts the other person on the defensive. His or her only response is to counter-attack or to lie down and die. Either way, you lose— even if you "win." Think long term by remembering the following:

- What is the ultimate good in this situation?
- What is the ultimate goal?
- Who do I need on board to make this decision work?
- How am I best able to affirm them, their idea, or their intention to move just one step forward?

You can do this even when you disagree. You can also do this when the other person is disagreeable. Buddhists believe you should not take personally the bad things others say to you or about you. They equate this negative behavior of others to that of a barking dog: Most people don't take the barking of a dog personally. Although it may be annoying, they simply say, "That's what dogs do—they bark!"

How about you? How are you affected by a disagreeable person? Do you take what he or she does or says personally, wasting valuable time and influence, when you could be engaged in affirming the other or helping him or her take the next right step? Nothing unnerves those who want power over you more than when you ignore their power struggle. If you never enter the ring, there can be no fight.

Here's What to Remember

Think of the enormous amount of time wasted in having a fight; holding a grudge; and thinking about the worries, the defenses, and bad feelings that follow. Try the following tips instead. The situation could be so different if you simply opt to recognize, choose, and affirm.

- Be mindful of your default habits with time.
- Seek to change your default habits with a focused activity.
- Experiment with different types of clarifying activities, from journaling to drawing to just sitting and thinking.
- Save time by considering the other's viewpoint before you do all the detail work.
- Balance the Three *A*s (ability, availability, and affability) when you work with others.
- Speak up at meetings.
- If you don't know what to say, listen and ask questions at meetings.
- Always pre-think a potentially conflicting dialogue. Practice good questions.
- Don't take anger personally; it stems from fear in the other person, not from you.
- Do the important things now.

Coach's Corner

Q: What are some ways to keep my list of things to do organized, but not so organized that I spend all of my time organizing?

A: When you take the time to organize, you never waste time. In fact, many successful people find that organizing, rehearsing, planning, thinking, and discussing actually help them accomplish more. Rushing head-long into projects will surely give you the illusion of being productive all the way until you hit a brick wall. The wall may be made of errors, unplanned-for problems, or even a wall of resistance from your team.

Plan your planning in the same way you plan your mealtime or an important appointment. Use your bonus time of commuting, sitting in a doctor's waiting room, or even during an airport delay as an opportunity to think through projects, decide an approach, or daydream your next big idea. These opportunities are abundant and often ill used with anxiety, pacing, and hurrying to the next thing. Use your time—don't let it get wasted.

Mindset Questions for This Chapter:

1. What are you noticing about your thinking about time just since the last chapter?
2. What have you done recently, even in a small way, that made more sense to you time-wise?
3. What else are you aware of that is happening in your life because of questions 1 and 2?

WORKSHEET 4.1

What Is Important, Really Important, to You?

1. What is your greatest value? How did you demonstrate it this week?

2. Who is most important person to you? What would he or she say you said or did this week that confirmed this?

3. What skill are you most proud of? How did you use it this week?

4. What is a good example of an act of courage on your part this week, however small it might seem?

5. What are three words you'd like on your tombstone and what are some examples of your living these words this past week?

Manage to Your Advantage

Ask the most important questions first

Prioritize the task that is closest to the bottom line

Manage tasks like email, writing, and meetings

STEP **5**

When you're starting a new project, no matter what your job is, you may feel like you're trapped in the classic Abbott and Costello routine: "Who's on first? What? Who's what?" Funny for them, but not so funny for you. You can free yourself by asking the most important first question: "Why?" The second question is then, "What's the desired outcome or result we want from this?"

The answers to these questions will apply to all of your tasks. They will help you answer the classic time management question, "Is this the best use of my time right now?" Sometimes, you may simply ask the question of yourself to anchor your thoughts. But most of the time, it is your right and responsibility to ask it of those to whom you report and those on your team. We've found that younger generations take more initiative with the "Why?" question than the rest of us. Perhaps it's because they've been brought up problem solving on the computer and are able to solicit answers on the Internet so quickly. "Why?" is an effective time management question because it prevents misunderstandings, backtracking, and confusion.

Think Like a Consultant

Getting on top of time and your projects means thinking like a consultant, especially at the beginning of a project. For consultants, the "Why?" and "Results" questions are a natural part of their selling process. They know they can't write a proposal or charge money for a project without a goal. They know they will not be awarded the business if they don't have goal clarity right from the beginning.

Once you've answered the "Why?" and "Results" questions, you can move to the more operational and practical ones, which, depending on your project, may include

- When is it due?
- With whom should I speak first?
- How many people are involved?
- What is the rollout process?
- What is our timeframe?
- What is the budget?
- Will a team be working on this?
- Where is this project priority-wise this quarter?

Maintain Sanity With Multiple Projects

Rarely do you have only one initiative going on at a time. For example, if you are a trainer and you're managing a corporate university or internal training calendar, you're probably developing a program for next month's release, meeting with vendors and suppliers, and working with your team on next year's budget. Keep in mind the following specific time management strategies for each of these common activities.

Prioritize Tasks

Start with the task that is closest to the bottom line. For example, if you are in charge of RSVPs for a training function, and especially if there is a high cost per capita for the program, checking RSVPs may be the closest task to the bottom line (or financial health) of your goal. Another example may be securing the right facility for an event. If it's important to book the cheapest facility early, then that task is closest to your bottom line.

Once you're satisfied that the most financially crucial tasks are completed, or at least at a stopping point, consider next the administrative tasks you dislike but are necessary to the smooth rollout of the project. Do difficult jobs first, when you are at your best and least stressed. Do lesser or redundant work when you're tired.

Manage Email and Phone Time

Following are 11 tips that can help you better manage your time when using email and making phone calls:

1. Set your email send and receive timing to only get email as often as you want it. If you're attempting to contact a lot of people by email, you can then plan when you'll tackle the myriad responses you're bound to receive.
2. Try to set definite times when you do not want to be disturbed, and tell those who work most closely with you or help you to serve your clients.

My best tip comes from Mark Twain: "If the first thing you do each morning is to eat a live frog, you can go through the day with the satisfaction of knowing that that is probably the worst thing that is going to happen to you all day long!" If you start your day doing the activity or task you dread the most, you will spend far less time and energy worrying about the task itself.

—Marcie Austen

Director, Human Resources

Shure, Inc., Niles, Illinois

3. Plan your outgoing telephone calls. Use a sticky note to jot down a phrase to help you reach your goal with the call, for example, "I need your help locating this product information by Friday at noon because it is key to the success of the new sales training webinar." Remember to use the words "need your help" and "key to the success of."

4. Have work right in front of you that you can do while you're on hold.

5. If you need to make regular calls to someone else, agree on a timeframe or day of the week that always works for both of you. Make a note in your database.

6. If you're attempting to set phone appointments with lots of people, suggest two that are good for you and add "or please suggest a few alternatives."

7. Leave clear messages on other people's voicemail. Always leave your name, phone number, and when you'd prefer they call you back.

8. Be clear about any time constraints up front. If you've ever worked with the media or public relations, you know that PR people are very clear about this. The rest of us can follow suit. "My deadline is Tuesday at 3 p.m." or "I prefer email to a phone call, please."

9. Always keep a pen and paper by the phone. This sounds so simple, but have you ever been without one?

10. Write the way people read. Take a lesson from the best newspapers. Use headlines. Make your key points jump off the page. Use bullet points, bold face type, italics, or anything that will make the points stand out.

11. Finally, analyze tasks that you keep putting off. Ask yourself questions such as, "Why is this not getting done? Is there some detail I'm missing? Was my judgment about the importance of this task wrong when I put it on today's calendar?" After a few times of pushing off a task, try to break it down into smaller parts and put them separately into the calendar again. Sooner or later, that task will become a series of tiny, easy-to-do steps, or you'll decide to rethink and remove it from your list.

Kick-Start Writing and Other Time-Consuming Activities

Time-consuming activities such as writing may be difficult. Depending on your job repsonsibilities, you may need to write frequently, but writing need not be a dreaded activity.

Just Get Started

Do at least a little something to get started. Once you start, it will be easier than you thought it would be. Don't feel you have to write linearly at first. Begin with a list of ideas, a dangling paragraph, or a "what not to do" list. Most of us find that once we get something started, a project ends up being much easier than we thought it would. And once something is down on paper, it gets very easy to see where the next step is.

Others can also inspire you; for example, you can email someone for his or her thoughts. Or take a quick survey and develop your theme from it. Read a few good articles on the topic and get inspired from other authors. You may even want to quote them in the opening paragraphs or later in your work.

Learn Where You Have Ideas

When you have a great idea, notice your location. Use this knowledge to kick-start your thinking if you hit a writer's block or need a beginning idea. Remember to take an idea-capturing tool (PDA, notebook, and so forth) when you go to your idea space.

My best time tip is one word . . . jogging. Exercise is how I maintain energy and the ability to focus my thoughts. While jogging, the exercise helps me keep my priorities straight
—*Mickey Smith*
CEO, Oak Hill Hospital

For many people, the kernels of ideas come when they're not officially "at work," but rather jogging, walking the dog, taking a shower, or on a flight from a conference. We've begun many of our books and articles this way. When this happens, honor the idea by jotting it down and returning to it when you've got a keyboard or notepad in front of you.

Get Ideas From Others

Some of your best ideas might come from others. One of our most popular articles, "No More Mr. Nice Guy," resulted from the "ahas" we received from a group of highly energetic, motivated female sales associates with a national cosmetic company. *T + D* magazine published it, and now, nearly 10 years later, you will find it all over the Internet. It must have hit a note with trainers everywhere. Imagine if you could accomplish similar notoriety within your organization by incorporating the wisdom of those you train. People love to hear their own words reflected back; they also like to see their names in print.

Notice what time of day ideas come to you. Are you a morning person? Then plan your creative work then. If you're an afternoon person, do your lesser tasks first and begin writing after lunch.

Exercise—no matter how brief—does wonders for my thinking and creativity. My favorite individual thinking activity is swimming, but a short walk outside or up and down the stairs does wonders for restarting my thinking as well.

—Howard Prager

Director, Lake Forest Corporate Education, Lake Forest Graduate School of Management, 2003–2004 ASTD National Board of Directors

Take breaks at times when you are low on energy. We once worked with an instructional designer who absolutely had to get out in her garden to take a break and think when designing technical training. Don't get worn out. If you feel fatigued and ideas seem "flat," it's time to stop.

Make Meetings Matter

The key to managing meetings it getting the pre-work and the post-work done in the right timeframe so that the face-to-face meeting time is used for its most useful purpose—the live interchange of ideas.

Team Meetings

Before a meeting, plan some time for discussing routine matters with your colleagues to avoid wasting time when the group is face to face. Try emailing them first and setting up a conversation time. Have the conversation on a phone conference instead of calling everyone individually. Use the meeting time to collect and record all the information you can as you receive it. Have you just heard about someone's birthday? Put it in your calendar. Did someone give you his or her cell phone number? Get that in the address book. Is there an update in the training schedule? Make the change now.

I have staff get-togethers every morning at 8:45. They last for 10 minutes or 20—depends. The wonderful thing about it is that we all start the day basically together knowing what one another is doing, we have a few laughs, and we come together as a team.

—*Kathryn Wiley*

Director of HR, American Bar Association

One-on-One Meetings

Many techniques will help you be more successful time managers in one-on-one meetings, such as

◆ Don't permit other people to rob you of your time. When you see time robbers approaching, say, "So sorry. Got to run."

◆ Stand when another person enters the room, so that he or she will also remain standing.

◆ If you see that a meeting has the potential to cover many topics, suggest a later meeting at your convenience.

◆ Consider walking with the person back to his or her office, talking as you go.

◆ If you have an assistant, agree to a clear policy about who can have access to you and whom he or she should assist.

◆ Set time limits for your discussion: "I only have five minutes, but I do want to talk with you about that. Is this OK with you?"

◆ Don't just chat. Get to the point, and then say, "OK, thanks, I'll get on that."

Here's What to Remember

◆ Figure out where to start.

◆ Think like a consultant—ask questions.

◆ Manage tasks methodically.

- Use email and phone time to your advantage.
- Make time management techniques your ally for writing.
- Find ways to make meetings work.

Coach's Corner

Q: My commute is long and unpredictable. Sometimes I am much too early, sometimes uncomfortably late. Early is good, but late is becoming really bad.

A: You answered your own question. Unless you are a confirmed gambler, opt always to be early so as to be on time. When you gamble with time, the same thing happens as it does in Vegas—the house always wins over time. And when that happens, we lose.

Inspire trust by being on time; inspire respect by being prepared; inspire confidence by being organized; and inspire cooperation by being interested in the other person first, last, and always. Unless you are a gambler at heart!

Mindset Questions for This Chapter:

1. What are you noticing about your thinking about time just since the last chapter?
2. What have you done recently, even in a small way, that made more sense to you time-wise?
3. What else are you aware of that is happening in your life because of questions 1 and 2?

STEP
5

Pay Attention to Your Key Contacts

OVERVIEW

Learn the value of pinpointing the few rather than the many

Keep in touch efficiently and effectively with your most important contacts

Help your staff and colleagues work strategically rather than tactically

STEP **6**

Although many professionals have a database of hundreds or even thousands of contacts, the strategic ones will target the few who really matter. When you target your efforts and your people, you will discover the key to enjoying a successful relationship that values the time, talent, and treasure you both will reap from your work together.

Consider three main targets when you think about time management and the key people in your work and life: your boss's boss, your key customer, and yourself. For each of these targets, an overriding principle to help you manage time is to not be consumed with pleasing. Pleasing may seem to be the best use of time at the moment. It certainly waylays discussion, conflict negotiation, and delving into deeper concerns. However, in the long run, it is less effective.

Here's what happens when you work only to please, according to experts we admire:

- ◆ You are what author and speaker Nido Qubein sees as engaging in transactional activities that lead to little progress.
- ◆ Both psychiatrists Alfred Adler and Rudolf Dreikurs regard pleasing as misdirected behavior. They recommend you work for what is useful instead.
- ◆ Dr. Ling Wu, an executive leader in the pharmaceutical industry, suggests you make the distinction between being seen as either a service professional or a leader.

Consider how to work for progress, in a useful manner, and how to be viewed as a leader as you collaborate with the key people in your work and life.

Focus on Your Boss's Boss

Many times we focus too closely on our own boss and don't pay enough attention to the boss our boss has. Your boss's boss is a vital target for you, because he or she will encompass all that is needed for your relationship to succeed with your direct boss. This is where the budget, the priorities, and the expectations flow from and to your own leader. Even when you work for a CEO, this person still reports to a governing board. Everyone has a boss, even when it appears they do not. Be cautious, though, that you are not working merely to please your boss or your boss's boss, to get on their good sides, or just to do what they tell you to do. Instead be useful, purposeful, and helpful in solving their problems.

Certainly you want to do a good job, but most bosses need more; they need help transforming chronic issues and problems into solutions that work. Even the most demanding, rigid, and authoritarian bosses want solutions. An error they often make is to think that only they have the solutions and others simply implement those solutions. This thought process is transactional, not useful, and ultimately destructive to leadership.

Following are some ways to use your time wisely with your boss's boss (and by so doing, with your own boss). The essential leadership skill here is learning how to lead the leaders.

To put it simply: Managing your boss's boss is much too important to leave to your boss alone. Consider what you can do:

Make yourself known. Find the time, the reason, and the opportunity to engage him or her in discussion about something personal. Link this interest with something you can relate to. Children always provide common ground. Even if you don't have any yourself, you once were one. Photos and artwork of hobbies, schools, favorite activities, vacation spots, or interests are usually on display in their offices. Take a good look and inquire.

Discover the challenging. At the next conference, lunch in the cafeteria, taxi ride, or coffee break, ask: "What is the most challenging part of being the CEO, vice president of finance, global affairs head, and so forth?" The answer, its depth, and its importance will surprise you. The boss's boss will feel complimented by your interest and your ability to engage in useful conversation that is different from the regular chatter he or she receives from those who work for him or her. Try to use this one question daily. If you want practice, simply ask anyone—every receptionist, lunch clerk, taxi driver, executive, flight attendant, and waiter—you encounter. You will find that each could talk for hours. Just listen.

STEP 6

Connect to engaging information. Subscribe to the *Harvard Business Review* and recommend it frequently to others when you find an article of interest. Believe it or not, many of your colleagues don't subscribe to this insightful publication, so your perspective becomes different and helpful, which makes you different and helpful as well. Subscribe to *The New York Times*, especially if you don't live there. This publication is full of interesting articles that you cannot find anywhere else. *USA Today* may be the stock and trade of traveling executives, but *The New York Times* catches people's interest when you email them a link to a related article. Go beyond. Look for, inquire about, explore, and research other periodicals that are out of the ordinary. What do Europeans read? How about academics? Ask and explore, then refer.

Get known at meetings. First, volunteer to become involved in important projects that have high value and are high profile. When you participate near the power, you can be a part of the power. Second, prepare your meeting participation. Will you summarize and paraphrase when the going gets tough? Will you dare to make a risky suggestion? Will you ask the question no one else wants to ask? Not so many years ago, after cuts to flight attendants and pilot salaries, the executives of American Airlines awarded themselves bonuses. How do you think the CEO of American Airlines would have responded if someone, maybe you, had simply asked at a meeting, "How do you think the unions will feel when they see our bonus packages in the headlines tomorrow?" Another example is the true story of a colleague of ours in the food industry. Years ago, she was brave enough to ask an all-male executive marketing team if they really thought that a football premium being considered for a Super Bowl snack promotion was gender neutral. Her speaking up got them thinking and they changed the idea—with successful results. Third, engage in and follow up with communications that stimulate the thinking of others. Be the one at the meeting to look down the road and see what others aren't taking the time to envision just yet. Use the "I had one more idea" technique for follow-up emails. Motivate others by offering "one more idea" after the meeting. This connective technique makes you and your ideas extremely valuable. It also gives you a legitimate excuse to continue to work with and through those who attended the meeting.

Live with risk. Don't play it safe. Toughen up your skin. Remember the old saying, "It is easier to beg for forgiveness than to ask for permission." One of our clients, a high-ranking administrative assistant in a large company, said, "I don't really want to ask for permission. Then my boss has to think . . . and that always causes trouble. He simply isn't good at it." On the rare occasions that he did object to what she had done, she simply apologized, used the "one more idea" technique, and then went on with life.

Acknowledge reality. Many great leaders believe firmly in the chain of command. This relationship you are developing is not one for gripes, complaints, or even too many compliments. It must be as natural as possible with you and your style as the "value add." Some direct bosses do not want this relationship. In that case, respect their wishes and be alert for how you can be an absolute best business friend and ally. Find out their goals and what is important to them. Be aware of the expectations of you and your team, and then do a superb job. An upwardly mobile vice president we know once said privately to her boss, the president, "I don't want your job . . . yet!" She went on to say she had more to learn from him and was aware that he, too, was moving on. What was the result of that one conversation? She secured her position as the next president.

Radio and television personality Earl Nightingale often said in his speeches that there are only three things needed for success: the value of what you do, your skill at what you do, and the difficulty in replacing you. Be incredibly valuable to your boss, and your boss will take you to the meetings where you will make your boss shine.

Communicate well (in all forms). Make your emails different from everyone else in your organization. Use the subject line to inform the reader of what is to come and what you want them to do with it; for example, "Conference Call Summary: Please Return with Comments." Make the first two sentences in every communication answer the reader's two key questions: What is this, and what does it have to do with me? In the conference call example, you could state, "Attached are the minutes from Tuesday's call on global training. Your review and comments in a return email by June 4 will help us move the ideas on to the VP level for budget approval." Realize that few will read the entire email. They will do what you do—skim and only read the first line of each paragraph and the closing paragraph. Write that way. Speak well and present well. This means omitting slang such as *guys* or *awesome* or *whatever*. Instead, substitute words your boss uses, such as *results*, *profits*, *energy*, *optimism*, *value*, and *decisions*.

Get out there. Make every presentation an event, not a data download. Have three things they will remember and keep those clear throughout, rather than focusing on the data. Listen to what is said and to what is not said. Paraphrase liberally to make sure you understand and demonstrate to them that you understood. Remember, listening is all about the other person—the receiver—not about you. One PhD we work with confessed he never really prepared much for shorter update presentations. He then went on to add that, "They don't really make personnel decisions at those meetings, do they?" (Meetings are actually the most frequent place where they make them.)

Remember—success is the goal. Contribute to that success and someday some new worker will approach you at the coffee pot and say, "What is your greatest challenge as an executive leader?"

Focus on Your Key Customers

Your key customers may number in the thousands, or they may be within your organization across the aisle from you. Who is critical for you to help and to serve? Who, when all is said and done, does your business depend on? Who is the key person or type of person who really "buys" what you have?

For some people, this may seem obvious. For others, it can be elusive. Consider this choice carefully. A scattershot approach to customer contact is not as useful or as effective as it once was. Mass mailings from the past are now replaced with targeted ones.

And focusing on "too many" can actually turn off the key customers you want most. So here's what you should do:

Avoid thinking generically about your key customers and stakeholders. As often as you can, think of the person, not "the people." Individualize your thinking and the way you reach out to your key customers. This goes beyond simple ways that you may personalize emails. It involves strategic thinking by you and your staff and colleagues. Ask yourself questions such as, "How does this customer think and feel? How is he or she influenced? How does he or she make decisions?" This is an important time and energy saver because you are investing in the time to get valuable information rather than just doing something that will result in a poor decision.

Know your customers personally. Even when you deal with a very large organization, work for individual relationships. President Lyndon Johnson was fond of reminding other politicians that every handshake was worth 250 votes. Individuals tell other individuals. One Illinois member of the U.S. House of Representatives spent every lunch in his office on his exercise bicycle calling random telephone numbers in his district back home, introducing himself, and asking and answering questions. Can you imagine the added contacts that emerged when those he called told their friends and families? Who would you immediately tell if your representative or senator called you? When was the last time that happened?

Identify who's the boss. Our customers are truly our bosses. They pay us, they sustain us, and they are the reason we are in business. They are whom we serve—despite the concerns they muster, despite their seeming unconcern for us, and despite the challenges they present. The more you put this priority front and center of every meeting with your staff, the more you'll use that time well.

Save time by spending it. Be very cautious about "saving" time. Like money, we save when we spend well, and we increase what we have when we invest properly. Be very, very cautious when you are under intense pressure or when you are forced to make an unanticipated decision. For example, because money and time are at stake for our customers, if we allow ourselves to panic we may immediately discount our price instead of speaking to our value. With our teams we can become too anxious with disagreements. Go inside yourself and refuse to let the pressure of the moment steal precious time from you. The early explorers Lewis and Clark made a decision about which river was the real Missouri halfway through their journey to the Pacific. Out of all of their men, they were the only two to choose correctly; all the others chose the other fork in the river. Not allowing themselves to be forced into a decision, Lewis and Clark called it right. They were, like we are, under a great amount of pressure. Be careful that the pressure you may feel from your boss, your customer, even your family not overshadow your own good judgment. You may be the one who is choosing the right river!

Prepare well. Neglecting proper preparation is easy to do, even for professionals. Make sure you invest your time in preparing, and you will save and use time later as a great reward. Plan for what you want or do not want, plan for things going well and for the unforeseen, and plan for success and anticipate possible failure. Be cognizant of what you want from your ultimate plans, what your customers "really" want, and what your superiors "especially" want. Many activities appear flawless in their execution, but in the long run fail to achieve significant goals. You can avoid the problems through planning and investing time well.

Talk face to face. Never miss an opportunity to ask one more question that allows you to gain first-hand knowledge of what the other person really thinks and feels. Imagine being a waiter or waitress and asking, "How's everything?" Your customer has the opportunity to say something but would most often reply by saying, "Fine." But what if you asked, "If I could do one thing to make this meal more pleasurable for you, what would that be?"

Would your customer be more likely to answer the second question with an honest answer and in greater detail? The first question is tactical, ordinary, and pedestrian. The other is strategic, genuine, and different.

Get the right data. Make sure the questions you ask really go to the heart of what you want to know. Evaluation is a skill and an art. Too often we waste our time with questions that give us scant information.

Help others advocate for you. You don't have to be a professional salesperson or a negotiation expert to ask for a referral, a favor, or a concession. When you speak with your customers, members, and stakeholders, ask for their help in specific terms. Tell them what you need from them and why. Use the words "I need your help" and "because" and "the reason this is important is . . ." often in your conversations with them. Ask and you will receive.

Pay attention to the time you spend. Be aware that there are times when being present in the moment is much more important than anything else. This is critical at home and at work. Watching your child's soccer game? Put away the Blackberry and let your calls go to voicemail. For a child, nothing is more discouraging than to search for parents on the sidelines and see them texting away. Be present and have presence. One without the other is just like not being there at all. It also applies to your meetings. When you are there, be there—fully, completely, and attentively.

Work your contacts. The old saying, "What goes around comes around," is as true today as it was in the past, perhaps even more so. Value your contacts and show them your true friendship by asking them what you can do for them. Every time you ask for a favor, make sure you ask what you can do in return. Every time you receive, make sure you give. Every time you take the time or they do, understand the value of the time.

Focus on Yourself

We often pay the least attention to ourselves. As time goes by, we can become the neglected one. When we fail to pay attention to ourselves, it is too easy to suffer the pain of discouragement that robs us of the energy we need to pay attention to what really matters.

Psychologists Adler and Dreikurs wrote extensively about this issue. Adler noted that if he were to select one personality characteristic to give to a child, it would be courage. He went on to say that with courage, one could combat life's greatest problem, which is fear.

Those around us with courage know fear but are not stopped by it. Courageous people simply say "yes" to the next step when they are confronted with problems. For example, while on vacation in Montana, Kevin overheard a heated discussion about a ranching problem in a local café. One Montana rancher said to another, "Yeah, that is a problem. We've got to do something about it. Heck, even if what we do is wrong, we ought to do something!" They both had a laugh and then began the process of moving to the next step.

Discouraged people think of problems, not solutions. They let fear hold them back and then make excuses. Paradoxically, these people suffer from unreasonably high expectations of themselves, some hold excessively negative opinions of themselves, and others become equally and unrealistically overambitious. Although they may feel discouraged, they can excuse themselves because of their good intentions, their lofty goals, and their clear understanding of what they could accomplish "if only." By staying stuck, they focus on the perfection they aspire to internally that eludes them in reality.

However, when you recognize that usefulness—not perfection—is the goal, you can be free to see faith, progress, effort, and contribution—all strengths and assets at work.

Imagine the time wasted on perfection versus the time well used on usefulness.

This is what distinguishes those who seem to accomplish a great deal in the same 168 hours of every week from those who don't. They may not have any special tools or techniques, assistants doing their bidding, or monetary advantage. Rather, they simply think differently because they feel differently. . . because they know something that others don't yet know.

They know encouragement.

Here's What to Remember

- Consider that everyone reports to or weighs his or her decision making in light of someone else.
- Every moment with any one of your key targets is valuable, so plan ahead on what you'll say.
- Think of your key customers individually so your time with them is customized.
- Speak up when you are with your key targets. Use the present to voice your opinion.
- Remind yourself that your customer employs you.
- Write and speak with thought and clarity. Your key targets notice. Always work to summarize, clarify, and secure understanding.

- Take time each day to encourage YOU! You are the tool others depend on. Keep yourself sharp, repaired, and ready.
- You have advocates to help you—ask them. Involve the "who" while you ask about the "what" and explore the "how" . . . together.
- In the presence of your target people, think "useful" rather than "pleasing."
- The time to get to know key people personally will always pay off. Always!

Coach's Corner

Q: I know you think I don't multitask, but I beg to differ. If you were in my life, you'd see me multitasking all day long. And I'm good at it. I want to be even better and faster. Even if you term *multitasking* to be *multifocusing*, I'd like your ideas on how to do it better.

A: You don't always have to take the coach's advice! The prefix "multi" is the problem here. We advocate that you focus, not multifocus, and that you task, not multitask. When we add "multi" we initiate problems. This causes us to sometimes get sloppy and often worse, anxious and distracted. Few can multifocus well. It gets to be even more of a problem when we have family, clients, and colleagues observing our attention to our technology and tasks and not to them.

It can also be addictive. Can you shut it off when you are at home? On vacation? When you are in a meeting?

Like any addiction, it is easy for any of us, even the coach, to ignore what might be a better path, though not an easy one. Kevin is addicted to Milk Duds. He knows they aren't good for him, but they are snackable, available, and "are they really that bad for me?" The same is true with regard to how we use our time, attention, and concentration and how we react to the demands of the day.

Yes, we do multifocus and engage in many tasks in rapid succession. The question is less how we term that activity than how we use the opportunity better.

Here are some ideas:
- ◆ Plan how you want to do the project—when and with whom. Electronic mind maps, flip charts, and white boards are great for this because they can be openly displayed in your office for you and all to see and comment on.

STEP 6

- Delegate early and often. Let your staff and your family make some mistakes along the way. Delegation is a skill of the senior executive mindset.
- Engage as many people as will be affected early and often.
- Predict problems before they happen. Be ready for them even if they never really happen.
- Evaluate on a small scale as you go. Don't wait until the end of the project. Evaluate each and every meeting.
- Seek advice from those in the know and those far outside. Each will help you.
- Volunteer when others won't, even if you don't have to. The experience will help you, and the added profile to your boss will help you, too.
- Offer help to those who give it to you.
- Rest and reflect or suffer the consequences. No one wants a boss or a colleague who is torn asunder by the work.
- Best practices can be noted and remembered before, during, and after each activity and project. This helps you do "more and better" each time.

Mindset Questions for This Chapter:

1. What are you noticing about your thinking about time just since the last chapter?
2. What have you done recently, even in a small way, that made more sense to you time-wise?
3. What else are you aware of that is happening in your life because of questions 1 and 2?

WORKSHEET 6.1

The Value of Purposeful Planning

After each bullet, write down the first event, person, or interaction that comes to your mind. Do this quickly. You'll have time later to contemplate your answers.

- Consider that everyone reports to or weighs their decisions in light of someone else. Who comes to your mind? _____

- Every moment with any one of your key targets is valuable, so plan ahead on what you'll say. What will you say?

  _____

- Think of your key customers individually so your time with them is customized. Who comes to mind? _____

- Speak up when you are with your key targets. Use the present to voice your opinion. Who needs to hear what from you?

  _____

- Remind yourself that your customer employs you. What would you do without your key customer? _____

- Write and speak with thought and clarity. Your key targets notice. Always work to summarize, clarify, and secure understanding. Think of an upcoming meeting; what needs to be clarified?

  _____

- Take time each day to encourage YOU! You are the tool others depend upon. Keep yourself sharp, repaired, and ready. What are you waiting to hear from yourself? _____

- You have advocates to help you—ask them. Involve the "who" while you ask about the "what" and explore the "how" together. Who is your greatest advocate at work? At home? At an upcoming meeting?

  _____

- In the presence of your target people, think of yourself as being useful rather than pleasing the group What would that look like?

  _____

- Taking the time to get to know key people personally will always pay off. Who do you need to know and who needs to know you?

  _____

Connect and Get the Most From Your Time

Recognize the importance of tending to your network

Be prepared to make connections where you least expect them

Use the art of conversation to your advantage

An old gardening adage goes, "The best fertilizer is the shadow of the gardener." This is the image we'd like you to keep in mind as you read this chapter—just as no garden can thrive without care, no network can thrive without constant attention. This chapter is about showing up, being there, and connecting. It is about communicating your value and helping others to do the same. Finally, it is about doing all this in a realistic timeframe that is appropriate to your work and life.

STEP 7

The best networkers seem to have a seamless plan that connects them to all sorts of people who can help them and whom they can help in return. Is it a plan or simply a way of doing, being, and knowing?

Take Deb, for example. A longtime association professional and now consultant in the publishing arena, Deb was widowed early in life. Over the years, she developed a reputation as someone who knows people. Having had many lunches with Deb over the years, we've watched her operate with admiration. The key is that Deb listens. No matter the conversation, and it doesn't have to be the most work-related of topics, Deb listens and then often comments on someone else she knows who had a similar experience and how he or she approached it.

Deb is also very quick on the follow-up. If she mentions she'll email you a name, you find it in your mailbox later that day. She generally answers email within 24 hours; if she doesn't, you can bet she's traveling on business in Europe, as she'll let you know later.

Deb operates with respect, efficiency, and caring. Her persona reflects that of a natural networker. She has learned to use time wisely. At lunch, she listens intently. She makes notes in a planner. She follows up quickly, and you hear from her quarterly—usually asking to meet for breakfast or lunch. These are simple things, but strategies that keep Deb in the know with those she knows.

The fertilizer that comes from the shadow of the gardener is not chemical or false or wrong; rather, it is natural, authentic, and right for the time and the plant. This is what the natural networker, like Deb, knows as well.

Recognize Your Perennials and Annuals

Like the gardener, we have perennials and annuals in our networking garden. (Perennials are those plants that come up every year, like daylilies, roses, and daisies. Annuals are often more noticeably colorful, like geraniums and marigolds, but die off in the colder weather. They need to be replaced next season.) Our connections are similar. Some, like perennials, we learn to check in with periodically, knowing they'll always be there with some amount of tending. Others, like annuals, are one-time contributors, fun for the moment to be developed quickly, but not worth intense time projecting into the future.

Connecting with people takes time, whether electronically or face to face. It's important to remember that electronic contact can still be personal contact. A key relationship builder is the timing factor; something good will happen either now or along the way. Too often, people put the business benefit ahead of the personal satisfaction of helping and connecting.

—*Nicole De Falco*
Business Communications Strategist
Owner of Write Influence: Saying What You Mean

Be Prepared—"Ya" Never Know Whom You Might Meet

We once attended a free after-work event sponsored by a major national newspaper for professional development in adult education—many of us were trainers, educators, and consultants in adult education. In return for the opportunity to tout its use as an educational tool for schools, the paper provided some speakers followed by a networking hour of wine tasting and hors d'oeuvres. It was overall a very classy event, gratefully attended by educators who are not frequently wined and dined.

But what we noticed in the networking hour surprised us. About 90 percent of the hard-working invitees were hunkered down in corners with friends they came with, hastily eating plates piled high with the free hors d'oeuvres. The mingling space in the center was empty except for a few lonely marketing representatives of the newspaper that sponsored the event.

It was clear that most people were not taking advantage of this great opportunity to network and connect. They were just hungry. How many times have we let opportunities like this slide by? Worse, we were actually wasting time when we could have been "planting seeds" and building our connections. (Note: It didn't take us long to locate a lonely newspaper marketing representative who was willing to take a look at a preview copy of our latest book. Nobody else was talking with her!)

Countless stories on this theme are revealed when you ask people, "So, how did you meet so and so?" Their answers are often very natural and simple, "Oh, at church coffee hour . . . or at a reunion . . . or at a neighbor's open house . . . " Life presents us with myriad events and situations to meet those whom we can affect and vice versa. We just have to take the initiative.

We call this the "Ya Never Know" theory. It means simply that connections happen when you least expect them to, and it's important to be prepared. Professional speakers will tell you that it's not the number of people in the room; it's having the right people in the room! Don't sell yourself short anytime you're out among others.

Harness the Lost Art of Conversation

Two thousand years ago, Latin philosopher Publilius Syrus wisely commented, "Conversation is the image of the mind. As the man is, so is his talk." Nothing reveals more to another about your mental framework than your ability to make conversation that is appropriate to the situation, whether at work or at play.

We've noticed that at weddings of young people, interaction doesn't begin until drinks are served. What a waste of valuable networking time. Think of the lines you stand in, the assigned seating arrangements you wait in, and all the other situations where conversation and connecting can occur. A social event can be a wonderful use of time—time when you can affect another. Think of your networking opportunities, events with cocktails and dinners for sure, but what about those awkward moments in an elevator? What if you were the one to introduce yourself and compliment someone on his or her outfit? Sometimes being respectfully playful yields much more than assuming an introverted stance. Find appropriate times to engage in conversation with a person in a check-out line, with your seatmate in an airplane, or especially when you are the only one invited to a dinner party who knows no one else seated around you. This is your time to network and to shine!

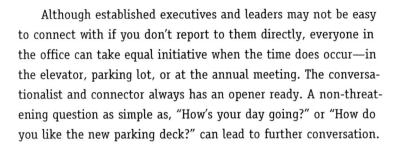

Although established executives and leaders may not be easy to connect with if you don't report to them directly, everyone in the office can take equal initiative when the time does occur—in the elevator, parking lot, or at the annual meeting. The conversationalist and connector always has an opener ready. A non-threatening question as simple as, "How's your day going?" or "How do you like the new parking deck?" can lead to further conversation.

So what does conversation have to do with time management? Everything! The networker who makes an impact listens well but also has planned questions that show his or her knowledge of the conversation partner's needs. From the wedding guest to the executive, the other is always more involved in his or her situation than ours. Once we can get them talking about what's on their mind, we can make mental notes as to how to follow up and build our network.

Social networking tools and viral marketing are valuable resources for keeping in touch with people we know, friends or colleagues of people we know who could become part of our network, and people we used to know. We can find people, seek out mutual interests, engage them, and discover new best friends. This can be a valuable use of time.

It can also become a significant waste of time. We have noticed that many professionals prefer to work on social networking rather than pick up the phone, visit a client or colleague, or handwrite a thank-you note. Social networking sites have their place in our lives, but they will rarely replace personal relationships. Being available and present for a friend or client is best done on site or over the phone by you with them, whenever possible.

Be aware of how much you use your tools and what they do for you. When you have spent a considerable amount of time emailing and visiting social networking sites, ask yourself two questions, "Is this the best use of my time right now?" and "What happened as a result of my activity?"

Recognize That the Medium Is the Message

We've been talking about the gardener and how the constant, caring attention to the garden is so important. When the fertilizer is wrong—too much or the wrong kind—disaster can result. The plants die. They are overwhelmed by poor choices. The same can happen to us if we're not careful of the messages we send while growing our network.

One of our colleagues recommended a friend with a book idea to his literary agent. The resulting connection was positive—the agent agreed to represent the friend and a nice publishing deal resulted. According to our colleague, the friend emailed his thanks for the referral and in addition sent a gift in the mail. So far, so good, right?

However, when the colleague opened the mailed gift, he was surprised to find himself the recipient of a corporate incentive-type, mass-produced item with the friend's company name and marketing slogan etched on it. So much for a personalized "thank you"!

Sociologist and philosopher Marshall McLuhan is well known for his work on the idea that "the medium is the message"—in essence, how our method of communicating affects the structure and intent of the message. How different the message of the gift would have been had it been personalized in some way? Contrast that with the gift another colleague sends to referrers: chocolates manufactured by a local religious organization that fights poverty—one that he supports and even mentions in his presentations.

Your Value and How to Communicate It in the Time You Have

It's about time . . . and more. When you network, you can easily become distracted. The phone vibrates, an email alert pings, you have less time than the person you are speaking to, you rush and realize it later, and you answered emails during a meeting only to find you missed the point being made at the meeting. Your value is communicated with the little things and the big things—it's just that people remember the little things more.

- Beware the myth of multitasking. You can only focus on one thing at a time. Too much multifocusing can waste precious moments that need more intent focus and create time-wasting anxiety.
- Try technology-free meetings. Simply try it once and you may never go back. Yes, it will frustrate some in your group, but as it becomes the norm, your meetings will be shorter and more purposeful.
- Turn off your audible email alerts. An alert is jarring and anxiety producing.
- Consider budgeting or scheduling specific email work times. In this way, you can devote quality time to your considered responses.
- Prioritize according to task, not according to your preference. Don't eat dessert first!
- Work a bit on the hardest task first. Just a bit, just 15 minutes . . . and then see what happens.
- The real secret is to review your folders regularly. Reviewing allows your brain to re-new.
- Your tomorrow list should be the last thing you do as you leave the office so it is off your plate and you can leave the office behind.
- When you make a mistake, pick up the phone. Few people view a sincere apology as a weakness or a mistake. In fact, when you apologize, they come to you.
- What is the best use of my time now? What action do I take next? And with whom? Absolutely the best questions ever. Thank you, Alan Lakein (author of *How to Get Control of Your Time and Your Life*).

Most people keep written note cards. They even file them away after displaying them on their office shelves for a while. An email is nice but fleeting, and the electronic medium bespeaks "quick, out of sight, out of mind." The written note or small gift is tangible, and the connection is as well. Taking the time to present your networking message with the right medium is always worth it in the long run.

Be Persistent and Have the Right Perspective

With respect to networking events and meetings, it's hard to know what to spend your money on these days. Sometimes "free" events are not really free but disappointing marketing ploys that sacrifice your time and deflate your attitude. Often, costly seminars and events disappoint; you leave knowing not much more than you arrived with. But ask seasoned connectors and networkers if they've experienced both and they will undoubtedly say, "Yes!" When your investment in time and money surprises you, take stock and move forward. Try a new group or association. Try meeting people before or after a meeting. Use the experience to write an article or blog.

If you seem to constantly miss opportunities at work, try a different tactic. Arrive earlier or stay later. Say "yes" to invitations you've traditionally turned down. Be alert to when the boss and other key people arrive and leave. Work with new hires. Help the administrative assistants. Volunteer to be on a task force. These are all potential connection opportunities.

Finally, persistence and the right perspective will pay off, and you'll be known as the natural networker among your friends and colleagues.

Here's What to Remember

- Let your shadow show frequently with those you want to affect.

- The simple tools to connect are often the best—voice, eyes, open-ended questions, and your 3 × 5 cards.

- Mind your method and medium of thanking and appreciating.

- Take advantage of every opportunity you're face to face—with anyone.

- Be a good conversationalist—prepared and listening. Tell a story and ask a question. Keep your talk to 60–90 seconds at a time so that you don't make the error of going on and on!

- Professional influence is achieved through the artful communication of value so that the audience, customer, or client trusts and continues to trust.

- Every successful relationship achieves a zone of understanding, a leveled awareness of each person, and the value of vulnerability is evidenced through questions.

- With a focus on active and intentional listening, the professional relationship is one that stays "on tangent" (not only "on target") so that through encouragement and enrichment, the relationship grows in new ways.

- Focus on the big effect of small talk with attention to emotional intelligence.

- "You are important in my life." A trust-building and appreciative close such as this lets the other know how much he or she is needed—as a person, a colleague, and a valued customer and partner.

Q: I travel for business and have a young family. How do I decide which comes first and when? More so, how do I then explain it to the ones in my life who come in second?

A: First of all, no one has to come in second. Everyone can feel first with focus. When you speak to someone in your life, really pay attention. Listen, engage, remember, and be completely in the present moment. Eckhart Tolle's *The Power of Now: A Guide to Spiritual Enlightenment* is a good primer.

Second, we've advocated planning. This is a good time to do more of it, even with all of the members of your life. Use a flip chart with crayons and involve your family. Involve your business partners and your inner self in constructing a mind map on ThinkBuzan.com (www.thinkbuzan.com/uk), or brainstorm and share your mind map through Mind Meister (www.mindmeister .com/content/product). If you prefer not to use a computer, drawing a colorful flip chart allows for collaboration. You can hang your masterpiece-in-process in your office, dining room, and so on. Every member of your family and staff can do the same. It will give them a sense of priorities, work responsibilities balanced with home, and allow everyone to see what is not on the sheet. (One of Kevin's clients was very proud of his mind map until a colleague asked, "And where is your family?" Needless to say, that was a moment of discovery!)

Third, don't be afraid to make choices and to live with them. You may have to miss a ball game; try not to miss a graduation. You might miss a dinner out, but don't miss a birthday. If you might be gone for an extended trip, plan a nightly Skype call to read the kids a bedtime story. Sending cell phone pictures or emailing daily postcards and updates reminds those who are important to you that they are never far from your thoughts.

WORKSHEET 7.1

Plan Your Next Connection

Kevin met Chicago's Mayor Daley on an airplane leaving Washington, D.C. It was a chance encounter. "Hello Mr. Mayor!" Kevin said. As Kevin prepared to converse and ask questions, the mayor immediately said, "Kevin, tell me about yourself." The conversation continued until both found their individual seats. Kevin hadn't planned the connection, but the mayor had! The mayor always focuses on the other person and takes the lead. It is his method of operation. Kevin forgot to do that and learned a lesson about planning how he would connect even in chance encounters.

Plan your next connection. Think of a connection you are likely to make in the next week.

- ◆ Who is this person? More important, who is this person to you? Why do you think you have singled him or her out for your special attention?

- ◆ What does he or she seem to care about, be interested in, have first and foremost on his or her mind?

- ◆ What question can you ask that will stimulate the other person's interest?

- ◆ What will you add to the encounter?

Three connection skills that will help:

1. Listen by paraphrasing rather than by adding things about you. Focus completely on the other person.

2. Question with lively interest to help the person talk more about him or herself.

3. Begin adding with the phrase "I really like what you said about _____ and that reminds me of _____."

Remember:

- ◆ You have to be genuinely interested in him or her, stay focused on him or her, and listen with a respectful curiosity.

Mindset Questions for This Chapter:

1. What are you noticing about your thinking about time just since the last chapter?
2. What have you done recently, even in a small way, that made more sense to you time-wise?
3. What else are you aware of that is happening in your life because of questions 1 and 2?

NOTES

Understand the Forces That Affect Your Use of Time and Energy

Keep your mindset aimed on energy and engagement

Recognize what you need to do when you are caught in the rip tide of life

Think before you do, and focus on outcomes

Time management is often seen as a way to save a minute here, another there, or to do things faster and more efficiently. Few books tell you to take more time, waste some here and there, and, in general, slow down! Efficiency is the goal, and conserving time is at a premium in the search for maximum effectiveness.

Don't Manage—Focus!

Time management often connotes control, authority, and molding time to our needs. You manage your time. How often do you attempt to do something that renders more time?

But what if you viewed your relationship with time less as management and more as a focus of your energy? You might then think of time differently and therefore interact with it differently. Rather than being anxious to save time, you could decide to evaluate not only the task before you but also the moment you are in and its ultimate significance in your life.

What if you saw time in the same way you see currents in the ocean or even the rip tides that swimmers become dangerously caught up in? When a swimmer, even near a beach, is caught in a rip tide, the first natural reaction is to swim—harder, faster, and stronger. However, that is the exact opposite of the appropriate and survivable response. The swimmer should instead go with the current, which allows the current to take the swimmer to where the current disperses, enabling the swimmer to move and swim freely back to the beach. That first panicked reaction of "I must fight to survive" is actually a response that may doom the swimmer to exhaustion or death. It is the measured reaction not to fight the current that allows the swimmer to live to tell his or her story.

Certainly time management is a worthy goal, and you and I can save minutes, hours, and even days with pre-planning, technology, and peer involvement. However, some situations demand that we go with the current, understand the forces around us, and live to "swim" another day. You can understand the difference by recognizing time not as a static entity but instead as energy, engagement, and encouragement.

◈ Energy is about you. Like the swimmer who makes it to shore, the best time managers use their own power with time rather than attempt to fight time. For these people, life is rarely rushed; they are seldom late; and they seem to be awake, alert, and alive. They have harnessed their energy.
◈ Engagement recognizes the time required between two people. We speak of the time prior to marriage as the engagement. This is seen as more than the day the couple met, although they certainly engaged that day also.

Energy and Time Relationship

Energy as it relates to time is
- a product of our awareness
- a decision we make
- an outcome we evaluate
- a beginning . . . again.

Engagement is not so much an event or a time period as it is a process together. The engagement with time you have is a dance with time. When you move correctly, when you see time as a partner, when you focus on the enjoyment (and not only on where your feet are), then you are free to move around the dance floor of life.

◆ Within engagement comes the valuable tool encouragement, which is a dynamic that creates something more between people located together in time. Often you spend time shaving, cutting, controlling, and feeling the demands of others as if you are in a kind of race with them. Perhaps you are racing, but encouragement helps you cheer them—and you—on during the race. Only one person is the ultimate winner of a marathon. To the many who race, however, winning is never their goal. They win when they finish.

◆ Focus is the calmer place in your life and work where you build in short breaks to think, not do. Focus on outcomes, where you want the project to go, what this next evaluation should accomplish, and what you most want in your life. Sometimes the best thing you can do with your time is to think before you do!

POINTER

Do prioritize, don't procrastinate, and always review what is pending!

—Catherine Zalusky
Chief Operations Officer
Ob Gyn Specialists of
the Palm Beaches
Palm Beach, Florida

STEP **8**

Figure 8.1 contains a way to think before you do. Consider the four circles. These circles extend our understanding of the forces that influence how we use our time.

FIGURE 8.1

Influence Cycles

#1
Goals & Traditions

Certitude vs.
Autocracy

Leadership &
Vision

#2
Personal Experience

Self-Assurance vs.
Arrogance

Competence &
Charisma

PLAN of ACTION
Profits
Purpose
People
Productivity

#4
Discussion and Dialogue

Communal Wisdom vs.
Group Think

Leadership &
Vision

#3
Professional Skill

Intent vs.
Mis-steps or Mistakes

Required Next Step

Circle #1 reminds you of what you know, what you believe, and what you are certain about. Everyone has a belief about learning, how it happens, how to stimulate learners, and so on. This is based on what you know by being taught. It is your science, your education, and your base. In short, it is what we are certain about. If you push it too much, close yourself to new research, or demand from others, you will become dogmatic, autocratic, and the world will pass you by as you fade into the world of history and tradition.

Circle #2 comprises what you learned outside of school. Your personal experience usually augments the certainty of your science from circle #1. Engineers use the same textbooks, and yet the products of their efforts are quite different from one another. Economists study side by side and then spend the rest of their careers debating with the famous, "On the one hand . . . ." What you believe is critical to your knowledge base.

Circle #3 is about your personal level of skill—your toolbox. Our skills, combined with our certainty and our experience, provide the first step toward our self-selected goal. Here we have movement.

And circle #4 is all about whom you will involve, how you will work with a team, and how you will allow the team to affect your certainty, your experience, and your skills.

The circles are dynamic, and they are critical to your use of time. In fact, try an experiment. At your next team meeting, keep this chart in front of you and pay attention to what people say, how they are saying it, and where it is coming from. Are they speaking from knowledge and research or from autocratic certainty? Do they seem self-assured from their experience, or are they simply arrogant? Do they seem to use their skills to make a solid next step, or do they hesitate? Finally, and this is a critical step, are they trying to convince others, or are they open to involving others?

> POINTER
>
> The derailment of a CEO is seldom caused by a lack of information about the latest technology in marketing, finance, or production; rather it comes about because of a lack of an interpersonal skill—the failure to get the best out of the people who possess the necessary information.
>
> —Kets de Vries

The central circle is the outcome circle. Here rest the profits, the purpose, the plan, the people, and the productivity. If that is not about time as energy, what is?

Here's What to Remember

- Banish the word "busy" from your typical response.
- If others pressure, and you feel backed into a defensive corner, thank them for their interest, ask for their help, and ask questions that will help them to think also.
- Be intentional with email.
- Prepare for your next voicemail and then listen to the voicemail you just left.

◆ Be on time every time. No excuses.

◆ Make sure your staff knows what is important to you. Share your personal mission.

Here are some additional tips to help you focus your energy. Bob Gilbert and Sean Hoffman co-direct the Ambulatory Services of OhioHealth, and they use the following techniques to focus the energy of their staff.

1. Respond to every voicemail and email within 24 hours, if only to tell the person when he or she can expect a full answer. You will be amazed at how cooperative your colleagues will be if you are prompt with them.

2. If you have a staff, your job is to summon the best from them, not do it all yourself. If you do not have a staff, your job is to bring the best out of those you meet with. You don't have to do it all yourself.

3. At the end of the day when you are greeted with, "How was your day?" talk about what you accomplished first, not what went wrong, not how exhausted you are, not that you don't want to talk about it. (Then watch how your partner responds.)

4. It is important with time and energy management that you work from a plan, not from your in-the-moment reaction. In the same way that Bob and Sean have a way to keep their thoughts front and center, you can also. For example, the next time you are on a conference call, take your four circles with you just to keep yourself on track!

Coach's Corner

Q: I know you advocate sending handwritten thank-you notes on a daily basis to be a better leader, to show appreciation, and to influence more. But really, who has time for that? Emails are faster, correct?

A: You have the time if you make the time. A huge time waster is email. You can barrel through your email and not make a dime or a dent in a project. Handwritten notes, personal phone calls, and a walk to another's office will always yield abundant results because of two things: it works and no one else does it. This is reason enough to be highly selective about using email.

Mindset Questions for This Chapter:

1. What are you noticing about your thinking about time just since the last chapter?
2. What have you done recently, even in a small way, that made more sense to you time-wise?
3. What else are you aware of that is happening in your life because of questions 1 and 2?

Focus on What Is Significant

Center yourself and your world for action

Go from thinking about being busy to thinking and doing things that matter (legacy thinking)

Adapt to others' pace to the extent that is helpful to you

The smile on your child's face as you attend his or her school play, your boss's energy while explaining the initiative both of you have crafted, the opening of the first rose of summer in your garden, and the completion of your retirement investment planning—all of these are your legacy. Each is a selected, targeted activity that is the result of more than simply checking off a box, attending a meeting, or deleting a file to do. Although each has its own priority and importance, each is also a fulfillment of sorts by someone who did more than make an appointment. These are the activities of a life well lived.

I believe in integrating your work, family, and pleasure— thinking of it as a whole, not separate parts. That would mean one calendar containing everything! That also would apply to, as they say, 24/7. I believe that takes the pressure off of having to perform things within certain time slots of the day.

—Janet Frazer, President
Janet Frazer and Associates, Training and Development
Consulting Firm
Palm Desert, California

STEP **9**

Center Your World for Action

"The eyes look out at the world, not under it, down at it, or away from it. So look squarely ahead . . . " writes British vocal expert Patsy Rodenburg as part of a warm-up exercise in her book, *The Right to Speak*. She calls it "centering," and it is part of an important series of mind, body, and voice alignments for the speaker—one that we use frequently with speaking students.

"Look out at the world" is an important habit not only for the speaker but also for the human being. Do we look out less and less at the world today? The following pointers are some observations from our colleagues.

POINTER

Waiting in my car in Chicago's busy downtown loop to pick up my child from a job interview, I counted that four out of five pedestrians who passed were connected to something electronic either in their ears or at their ear—blank looks on their faces, oblivious to the world around them.
—*A parent/chauffeur*

POINTER

Walking among myriad travelers at O'Hare airport, most looking down while discussing something on their cell phones, I wonder how they find their gates!

—*A frequent air traveler*

In refreshing contrast, old Polish and Russian couples and groups of friends walk together along the sidewalk paths of Lake Michigan on summer mornings. All they do is talk, with hands clasped behind them, looking out at the world every day. Their faces are animated—always.

Along the same lake paths are also those urbanites seated alone on park benches, looking out at the ever-changing lake. Often they'll occupy the spot for an hour or two, sometimes reading, but most often not. If they're not centered yet, they certainly seem to be headed that direction.

Many people have made major life decisions after days, weeks, months, and years of work determining how they perceive the world around them. Although more time consuming in that it involves concerted observation to analyze and change it, this method of action taking is rooted in calm.

Develop Legacy Thinking

"Well, day, what will I do with you?" a retiree we know asks herself early in the morning each day. Faced with a new life without work outside the home, she told us she began asking that question out loud to buoy her spirits. She found that it worked. This is a great example of what we call legacy thinking.

Legacy thinking involves how we use the waking hours we're given to do what matters most. Legacy thinking is healthy for the mind and the morale because it naturally gears us to what is important. Great leaders and thinkers are either born with or have worked hard to develop their legacy-thinking abilities. We can all align our thinking to legacy thinking—with a little "surgery."

POINTER

Walking my dog on a Saturday morning, I observed not one, not two, but three young fathers out with the baby in the stroller. The baby is laughing, pointing, and looking ahead, yet the father doesn't notice; he's talking or texting on his phone.

—*A middle-aged urban mom*

POINTER

We are what we think. All that we are arises with our thoughts. With our thoughts, we make our world.

—*Buddha*

Use the Thought-Replacement Technique

Consider a surgical technique we call thought replacement. These days we have hip replacement, heart replacement, and shoulder replacement. Why not do surgery on our thoughts? The same approach applies:

STEP 9

- ◆ Diagnose the ailing thought that is no longer useful. Consider those thoughts that give you pain due to the emotional chaos they cause. Ailing thoughts mire you in bad habits. They move you to negativity. They stop you in your tracks.

- Identify the thought that will serve you better.
- Remove the old thought. Here is where replacing a hip and a replacing a thought are most different. The hip is replaced once. The thought needs to be replaced frequently: daily, hourly, or perhaps even minute by minute.

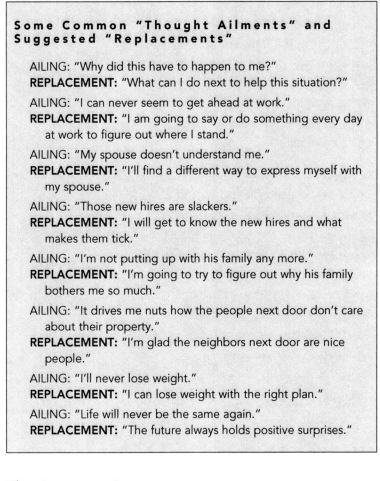

Some Common "Thought Ailments" and Suggested "Replacements"

AILING: "Why did this have to happen to me?"
REPLACEMENT: "What can I do next to help this situation?"

AILING: "I can never seem to get ahead at work."
REPLACEMENT: "I am going to say or do something every day at work to figure out where I stand."

AILING: "My spouse doesn't understand me."
REPLACEMENT: "I'll find a different way to express myself with my spouse."

AILING: "Those new hires are slackers."
REPLACEMENT: "I will get to know the new hires and what makes them tick."

AILING: "I'm not putting up with his family any more."
REPLACEMENT: "I'm going to try to figure out why his family bothers me so much."

AILING: "It drives me nuts how the people next door don't care about their property."
REPLACEMENT: "I'm glad the neighbors next door are nice people."

AILING: "I'll never lose weight."
REPLACEMENT: "I can lose weight with the right plan."

AILING: "Life will never be the same again."
REPLACEMENT: "The future always holds positive surprises."

The Recovery Process

After any surgery, a fairly regimented recovery process typically involves rehab, check-ups, and lots of love and patience on the part of the patient and the caregiver. Thought replacement recovery is much the same.

◆ Rehab: It's important to keep on track using the new thought as much as possible in real, applicable situations. "Use it or lose it," as the saying goes.

◆ Check-ups: Ask your caregiver (neighbor, friend, partner, parent, child, co-worker) how you're doing. Has your behavior changed to reflect the new thought? Check in with yourself as well. Your relationship with yourself is important. If you're not honest with yourself, with whom can you be?

◆ Continued patience and love: Remind yourself that behavior change takes time. Habits are known to take 21–30 days of struggle to change. Some of this research comes from Dr. Maxwell Maltz, who wrote the bestseller, *Psycho-Cybernetics*. Originally a plastic surgeon, Maltz noticed that it took 21 days for amputees to stop feeling phantom sensations in the amputated limb. Steven Aitchison, a time scholar and blogger, writes, "When you want to start a habit, don't tell yourself you are doing it for life; tell yourself (your conscious brain) that you are going to try it for 21 days, and you'll often have more success."

> POINTER
>
> You've just got to work with yourself.
>
> —Freda Adcock, Cyndi's mother

Adapt to the Pace of Others

"Marching to your own drum" can be a detriment when you're managing time with other people, whether family members, co-workers, children, or distant relatives. Throughout life, we have ample opportunity to monitor our pace. Some periods in life seem to dictate fast pace and chaotic decisions. Others are more relaxed. Some people in life do the same—inspire either calm or chaos. It is

important that we find our own drum to march to but change the rhythm according to the song we're playing and the band we're in at the time.

Whether you're at home or at work most of the time, you're affected by how others want to do things. We all seem to be raised differently in this respect, and the true irony of life is that we often come to live and work with those who use time in the opposite manner as we do.

Listen First

Listening to the pace around you is the first step to adapting effectively. If you're a new employee, this is especially important.

◆ Notice if people are on time for meetings and if meetings go overtime.

◆ Observe the length of time the leader has the stage in comparison to everyone else.

◆ Listen to conversations to get a feel for what people are concerned about related to time—deadlines? Project teams? New leadership challenges?

◆ Watch your boss, especially making note of his or her arrival and departure times and attitudes.

It's also important at home and in your personal life:

◆ Notice how your children do things differently.

◆ Observe your roommate or significant other at the beginning and end of the day. Is there a difference in how time is used, or is it much the same as you?

◆ Does having a pet or a dependent person change how time is used at home?

◆ Watch how the oldest person in your household does the simplest things. How would you describe the pace? What can you learn from it?

Ask Next

Asking questions about why things are done in a certain manner in a certain timeframe is very important, especially when you are new in an environment. People adopt a time culture that is most often not written down anywhere.

- When do you expect me to arrive?
- When on Tuesday is the deadline for this?
- How do the interns typically use their day?
- Is tardiness a taboo here?
- What would you like me to do if I am running late?
- I noticed you shut your door in the morning. Am I allowed to interrupt you?
- When does catering typically arrive to set up the coffee?

Again, it's also important to ask in your home:

- When do you want dinner?
- How can I help you get ready the night before?
- Is there a reason you're all late to dinner?
- Can I help with that project so it doesn't take as long?

Adapt Accordingly

If your life includes a significant person with a fast pace of doing, thinking, and reacting, appreciate this and try to match it when you can. However, when you sense you're out of control or unsure of why you're doing what you're doing, stop and think. Take a moment to look at what you're both doing. Does it make sense time-wise?

Similarly, if your life includes someone who operates at a slower pace, how does this affect you? How can you learn from it and talk about it? Because we've all had different parents and cultural, regional, and environmental backgrounds, we'll have to learn to adapt to how we use time . . . until the end of time! If we can keep communication open and observation on track, we can build a comfortable pace into our lives every day.

Time cools, time clarifies; no mood can be maintained quite unaltered through the course of hours.

—*Mark Twain*

(1835–1910)

One thing that will help your time spent with others, save you time, and invest your time wisely is encouragement. In a nutshell, there are four skills of encouragement. In Table 9-1, you'll find each skill presented with a defining statement of belief, some behaviors that get you ready to use the skill, the skill itself as an empowering movement forward, and the contrary skill that helps you identify when you are not practicing the skill.

TABLE 9.1

The Four Skills of Encouragement

Pilots use a checklist before every flight. Experienced pilots use the same checklist *every single time.* More and more physicians are also using a checklist to make sure that procedures are perfect *each and every time.*

We can too. Encouraging others is a skill like any other. It will work when it is done well, and we can ensure that we do it well by having our own checklist that we review *each and every time.*

Knowing who we want to be (i.e., competently confident) and knowing how to prepare for it (prep behaviors), how to use the skill (empowering behaviors), and how to be on the watch for the usual ways we diminish ourselves and others (contrary behaviors) will all ensure that our skills are not haphazard attempts to do the best we can. We can get it right *each and every time.*

As you review the following four steps, help yourself become aware of what you are already doing very well and how you might also improve, sharpen your focus, or do a 180-degree turn.

1. Competent Confidence

"I am ready to do what is required as well as 'the more' that may be asked of me."

Prep Behaviors (readying oneself):

    Knows the data cold

    Greets others warmly

    Focuses on mutuality

Table 9.1, continued

Empowering Behaviors (the skill):

   Knows self (what works for me or what I need to learn)

   Understands value (as defined by self and other)

   Figures out what is needed (in "this" situation for "this" group)

   Understands how others are similar (and how they are different)

   Uses appreciative inquiry (what am I doing well right now?)

Contrary Behaviors (normal ways we diminish ourselves and others):

   Fights the new role

   Fears the reaction of others

   Freezes under pressure

   Flees tough meetings and interactions

   Flops long term . . . and waits!

2. Firm and Flexible Boundaries

"I give myself permission to do what is needed in the moment with an eye toward the future."

Prep Behaviors (readying oneself):

   Recalls previous needs, discussions, challenging issues, and questions

   Consults with experts and supervisor ahead of time

   Pre-plans for the tough questions . . . and the tough conclusions

Empowering Behaviors (the skill):

   Flexible with goals (especially cognizant of individual and departmental goals)

   Understands the "product of the product" (through pre-interviews)

   Understands the team model of collaboration (we not me)

   Uses assertive messaging with understanding (for how others think and especially how they feel)

Contrary Behaviors (normal ways we diminish ourselves and others):

   Rigidity in my personal agenda

   Self as technical expert only

   Obvious anxiety with unplanned questions displayed as reticence or arrogance

   Aggressive messaging with an attitude

   Waits!

3. Selective and Effective Communication

"I am prepared to adapt as needed for my colleagues with a significant message of worth."

Prep Behaviors (readying oneself):

> Practices effective communication daily
>
> Maintains awareness of one's own behavior that helps (and that hurts) good interactions with others
>
> Willingly seeks peer feedback with openness and nondefensiveness

Empowering Behaviors (the skill):

> Establishes relationships with others focusing on connection
>
> Shows obvious and clear interest in the other person
>
> Asks open-ended questions (questions that cannot be answered with a simple "yes" or "no")
>
> Uses "tag and add" technique to couple with the other's concepts and interests
>
> Ends sessions with encouragement ("I like . . . I appreciate . . . I look forward to . . . ")

Contrary Behaviors (normal ways we diminish ourselves and others):

> Nervously over-talks, arrogantly dominates, or shyly remains distant
>
> Does not ask questions or asks closed-ended questions
>
> Self-thinking or self-focusing
>
> Waits!

4. Invitational Initiative

"I take control over what I have control of. I will work to influence that which I have less or no control over."

Prep Behaviors (readying oneself):

> Plants seeds strategically and freely
>
> Secures added traction with seemingly small agreements
>
> Finds opportunities to invite partners along the way

Empowering Behaviors (the skill):

> Looks for unexpected opportunities
>
> Teaches with patient understanding
>
> Looks often for first steps everyone can take
>
> Follows up in a timely and systematic way

Table 9.1, continued

Contrary Behaviors (normal ways we diminish ourselves and others):

Contrary Behaviors (normal ways we diminish ourselves and others):

Shows up

Spits it out

Leaves

. . . and waits

. . . and judges

. . . and hopes or forgets

. . . and waits!

Here's What to Remember

- Look out at the world.
- Center your consciousness.
- Comment, visualize, or document what you see.
- Get rid of ailing thoughts by replacing them.
- Use a recovery process to keep new thoughts healthy.
- Listen to the pace of others first.
- Ask questions to help you adapt to the time culture.
- Think legacy to focus on what matters.
- With your thoughts, make your world.

Take the Next Step

You've gained an awareness of the world around you and commented on it. Isn't that enough? Perhaps. It's up to you to take the next step if you want to turn calm and comment into action. See how centered you really are by answering the questions in Worksheet 9.1. If you find that you aren't as centered as you thought, try the tips in Worksheet 9.2 to get you there. For the creative person, this is often more natural—finding myriad potential conclusions in simple observations. For the less creative soul, taking the next step may involve concerted journaling, coaching, or counseling to head in a new direction.

WORKSHEET 9.1

Are You Centered?

Can you tell if you are centered? Have you tried unplugging and "looking out at the world" every day? Answer the questions in this worksheet to determine if you are centered or not.

1. Do you check your PDA or phone for messages before you get out of bed?

2. Is it impossible for you to drive your car without a GPS or radio?

3. Do you momentarily panic when you can't find your Bluetooth device?

4. Are you unable to hold a conversation longer than three minutes without checking your phone?

5. Do you frequently forget where you've just been (on the road, sidewalk, or elevator)?

6. If your partner mentions what a nice day it is outside, do you know what he or she is talking about?

7. Do you say "hello" to someone before you say, "Got your text . . . "?

8. Did you hide behind your digital camera or phone at the last three family events?

9. Have you forgotten the names of other dogs on your dog-walking route?

10. Have you forgotten how to give directions using basic body gestures?

If you've answered, "yes" to most of these questions, perhaps you should wake up and smell the roses. Get in touch with the world around you—the people, scenery, weather, pets, and and all the other things beyond your electronic devices.

WORKSHEET 9.2

Ways to Get Centered if You're Not

If you know you're not centered, here are some tips to help get you there.

- Take a lesson from the criminal justice professional and identify the environment you're in at the moment. Who's on the elevator with you? Who is walking their dog every morning in the same direction? Has the hedge grown in the last week? Does your administrative assistant have a new hairstyle? Make more frequent mental notes of your world.

- Say "Hello" to everyone you deal with before the deal begins. This includes the coffee shop clerk, the dry cleaner, the teenage child, and the significant other. A simple "Hello" will sometimes open up situations that affect the deal.

- Turn off and put away the electronic and wireless tools for a time. The amount of time is up to you and how centered you want to get. It's very easy to QUIT the email function for an hour. During this time you can actually . . . think!

- Take a lesson from the naturalist. Every year the Audubon Society sponsors a bird count day. On this day, naturalists and bird enthusiasts simply observe and record the number and type of birds they see in a designated locale. The point is to see which birds are losing ground and which are multiplying and also to learn their migration patterns and lifestyle. This is not achieved by watching YouTube videos.

- Comment on what you see when you're centered. Write about it, talk about it, or visualize it in photography, art, or other media. The artist doesn't get to be an artist by rushing around. The playwright must center on life to recreate it. The instructor's best lessons are entwined with personal experience. The author's best quotes are his or her own.

Mindset Questions for This Chapter:

1. What are you noticing about your thinking about time just since the last chapter?
2. What have you done recently, even in a small way, that made more sense to you time-wise?
3. What else are you aware of that is happening in your life because of questions 1 and 2?

Make Time Your Friend

Stay in the driver's seat

In the same way that gasoline in your car's tank provides the energy for you to run the motor and reach your destination, time serves a similar purpose. The gas is not in the driver's seat; rather, it is safely hidden to do its only job. Time requires the same understanding. Time is never the driver, only the driver's resource.

Use Awareness, Understanding, and Choice to Stay in Charge

Earlier in this book, we wrote of self-regulation as a key ingredient in all of time management. In the end, it is your choices, your will, and your responsibility to be in charge of yourself. This is no easy task for sure, and one that goes on for the rest of your life.

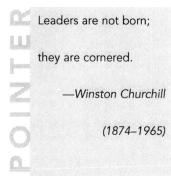

Leaders are not born; they are cornered.

—Winston Churchill

(1874–1965)

STEP **10**

Three qualities that will keep you up front driving the car are awareness, understanding, and choice.

Awareness

Loyola University professor Allan Schnarr teaches, "Awareness is a great gift." With ever-expanding awareness, you literally put yourself more deeply in the world with others rather than protected in your own shell from others. As a result, you exercise more control, flexibility, and responsiveness simply because you see, hear, smell, feel, and even taste the outer world. The more awareness you have of the outside world, the more you will experience awareness of the inside world.

Understanding

With awareness comes understanding, but only if you are curious. Renie McClay, a trainer and author who is an expert on culture, advises a curious approach to life—especially when you are most tempted to judge or disapprove. Her advice can be summarized with the following inner questions: "I wonder why they do that? I wonder how that came about? I wonder?" It's easy to instead pronounce, "That's weird!" One question asked with curiosity leads to the potential for expanded understanding. A statement leads to the dead end that self-certainty often brings.

Choice

With an expanding awareness and a deepening understanding spawned by your curiosity, you can now act. You choose the skills and tools to move forward one step at a time. Certainly not as simple as this paragraph makes it sound, but personal choice is truly your ultimate control. You choose to cooperate or to fight, to compete or to withdraw, to watch or to be involved, to enjoy or to endure, or to partner or to go alone.

Recently, I was out of the office for an entire week for a professional development course. Before leaving, I made sure I let all the key players in my typical day know that I would be away and who they might contact in my absence. I placed an out-of-office memo on my email and changed my voicemail message. Everyone knew how important this course was to me. When I returned, I noticed that work had been delegated in my absence and meetings covered. I find when I can truly be "present," I feel more energized, focused, and perform better. I can actually get my work done more efficiently—leaving more space for me to balance everything else.

—Amy M. Lakusiewicz
Sales Training & Development
Bayer HealthCare Pharmaceuticals

In any choice you make, for good or ill, you are the choice maker. And with your time choices, you decide, although it often doesn't feel that way. When pressed with the heavy seas and dangerous rip tides of life, you may too often choose to react and fight rather than think and then respond. These patterns develop early in your life. They help you make sense of the world, and they either work well or they don't. Even when they don't work well, however, your well-established patterns keep arising. Like trying to give up a favorite food, you can be beckoned back again and again—for just one more bite. Recognize those old familiar choices and create new responses when necessary.

Here's What to Remember

- Decide to decide. Waiting is only an option if it is part of a larger plan to move. Decisions help us go.
- Determine what is important to you.
- Acknowledge you live in a world with others who are remarkably different from you.
- Develop strong relationships with those whom you choose.

STEP **10**

- When you can, cooperate with your colleagues. When you find that cooperation is not an option, decide what you will do next.
- Burn very few bridges. When you burn one and regret it, remember you can reconstruct it from your side of the river.
- When you encounter the unusual, be curious with wonder.
- When you are lost, behind, or overwhelmed, don't keep driving—pull over and ask for directions.
- Abandon self-certainty—seek usefulness, otherness, and the next right step.
- Finally, always ask yourself: What is the best use of my time—right now?

Coach's Corner

Q: I know other people's lack of planning should not constitute an emergency for me, but what about my boss or my boss's boss? Sometimes a command performance does mean my stuff goes on the back burner—yes?

A: Yes. But that does not mean their anxiety over their lack of planning must become your anxiety. When they pass the baton, receive it with the skill and perspective you have. Carefully align what they want you to do, how you can help them, and then give just a bit more. That is what they really want.

Q: I find that I frequently underestimate how much time it takes for a team to "get it" when we are working on a project. Any hints would help. I truly believe projects can be done faster and better than most of the teams I'm on.

A: The secret word here is "most." If most of the teams you are on seem to be slower than you, then you might want to consider your expectations. When others, especially teams, feel you are disappointed in them, or angry, or impatient, they will tend to behave like sixth graders and go even slower. They do this not out of revenge but out of discouragement. In essence, the group think is saying, "I know we aren't very good . . . even you think so!"

Here are some quick ideas to save time when the team is letting you down:
- Only encourage. For the first month, only note progress. When failure or delay looms, you be the one to point out the "good side" of the effort being put forth, the

---

118 Make Time Your Friend

incremental progress, or the value of not having made some decisions that would have led to total failure. Stick with it for a month and then recognize what changes.

- Acknowledge progress with an opening question. Begin every meeting with the question, "Since the last meeting, what have each of you noticed that has been better or different?" Make them tell you out loud, make them stick to "better or different," and then summarize what you heard. This is powerful stuff, so be ready for what comes your way.

- Use email or a phone call two days prior to each meeting. Ask the attendees what they would most like to obtain from this meeting, what is vital, and what they need. This will help them focus and equip you with what you need to help them. Few things are more discouraging than an irrelevant meeting.

- Use a post-meeting email. After each meeting, send a summarizing email, but personalize the first paragraph for each one you send. Take the time to note progress and show your appreciation.

- Do not neglect the power of personal, handwritten thank-you notes. This is a key to enhancing relationships with discouraged people. Be selective and, over the course of a few months, hit everyone with a sincere, real thank-you note that cites specifics.

- Work to tone down your own perfectionism by seeking feedback about how others think the team is progressing. As with all improvement, begin with thyself!

Q: My kids play soccer, we travel for soccer, and we pay big money for soccer. I want them to belong, and I enjoy going to the games, but it seems a tremendous waste of time for me to stare at game after game when I could be working. I tried working on the sly once, but my kids noticed! Help!

A: When you are there, really be there. When you take a break to work, simply tell them that is what you are going to do. If you must take a phone call or respond to an email during the after-game pizza party, do so in the bathroom . . . few will follow you there!

The point is not to advertise that you are so important, so busy, so dominated by work, or a boss that you can't enjoy family time.

How about letting voicemail take the call? That's what it's for. If your boss mentions a call went to voicemail, don't apologize or explain; just pick up the voicemail in an appropriate timeframe and return to the work. Unless you are a physician with a life in the balance, do you really need the device on all the time?

Q: Is it possible to go on vacation without a computer, phone, and Blackberry?

A: Yes, but only if you want to! Announce it to everyone at work, find a vacation spot with terrible reception, delegate ahead of time, and go cold turkey. There is nothing quite so great as a vacation without the devices—once you are past the first 24 hours!

Q: In my office environment, there is one Chatty Kathy colleague who takes to heart your advice of not sending emails. Instead, we spend a lot of time in face-to-face conversation—time I could use more efficiently on task work. Any advice for how to keep face time to an appropriate amount without coming across too brusque or abrupt?

A: You can take one of at least three options here. Tell her. I'd begin, of course, with affirming your work together, your positive feelings for her, and the importance of the work you both do together. Then begin with, "I want to ask you for a favor that would help me a lot." Wait for her response. Then proceed, "I'd like for us to find a balance where we can still work together one-on-one and face-to-face but also with some of it by email. I find I could use the time, and it would provide both of us with a written record of our work together." A second option is to find a regular time each day or week for your one-on-ones. You'll have to enforce this one at the beginning with, "Kathy, can we put this one on our agenda for our regular meeting this afternoon?" Finally, one of my clients has a cube and has two signs, which he alternates as needed. One says, "Come on in!" and the other says, "I need some alone work time. Can we meet a bit later?" The point of all three is to speak up. Don't suffer in silence. No need to be nasty; in fact, if you don't speak up soon, it might get nasty.

Q: You've talked about how phone etiquette is important. Can you share some quick tips for how to come across more professionally on a phone call with a supervisor or client? For instance, how do I initiate or end a call gracefully? How do I handle it if the timing is off for a productive conversation?

A: When the time isn't right, let the call go to voicemail. Have you ever had someone answer and say, "Can I call you back? I'm busy right now." (Why did you answer it in the first place?!) Another approach is to time the interaction. When someone says, "Do you have a minute?" simply say, "Actually, I only have two minutes right now but will have more later. What would be best for you?" Then enforce it. Don't let them, even your boss, go overtime. A third approach is to get up as you finish the meeting with an explanation of where you are going that links to the person's agenda so that the "permission" will be easier to get. Finally, use two techniques the talk show hosts use consistently. One is to notify the person of the time. "I've got to run in two minutes, but first I want to ask you just one more question. Would that be OK?" (In effect, they are saying OK to your asking a question and to the two-minute time limit.) A second option is to get them off of the social talk and onto the business. "I love Colorado, too. Let me ask you one question. I know our time is limited here. I have only five or six minutes until I have to meet with John from accounting. Given the data we spoke about, what can I do today at this meeting that would be most helpful for you right now?"

Q: What is the best question you've ever heard about time?
A: Alan Lakein's question was, "What is the best use of my time right now?" Ask this question routinely, and it will keep you on track . . . as long as you listen carefully to the answer within you.

WORKSHEET 10.1

Personal Diary

Here are the questions you can ask yourself to see if you've made time your friend:

1. When is the last time that time was your friend? Recall an event where you luxuriated in your time with a project, a friend, your family, or yourself.

2. Recall a time when, under the gun, you won a race with time for a worthy cause.

3. What do you most appreciate about the time you have, however fleeting it might sometimes seem?

4. Recall a moment when you became aware of being in a fight with time, and you were able to change your mind about time.

5. What do you know about your use (and abuse) of time that you have to remind yourself to use time better each day?

6. Who is the most important person right now (at home and at work) whom you have to make more time for?

7. What is your first signal that you are on the verge of wasting time at home, at the office, or in the car?

8. What do you know for sure that will put you on the right track to making time your friend?

Mindset Questions for This Chapter:

1. What are you noticing about your thinking about time just since the last chapter?
2. What have you done recently, even in a small way, that made more sense to you time-wise?
3. What else are you aware of that is happening in your life because of questions 1 and 2?

NOTES

STEP 10

Capabilities Profile and a 90-Day Plan

Time is important when we have a job and when we want another job. Make a great first impression by adding two features to your resume: a capabilities profile and a 90-day plan.

Adding these two features to your resume conveys more than just a message about who you are; it conveys how you think, how you work, and how you will contribute.

And it will save you and your interviewer time. One thing you never want to do with any person in a senior position is to waste his or her time. Having a resume, a capabilities profile, and a 90-day plan usually results in the interviewer saying, often aloud, "How could I hire anyone else?"

Resumes tell what you have done. The capability profile tells what you can do. The 90-day plan says what you will do. Each, in its own way, burnishes your image. But too many times, people use the resume only as a look back.

Capabilities Profile

Here are some examples of elements to include in a capabilities profile:

- As a result of professional experience and academic training, enjoys a broad and in-depth knowledge of diverse customer business environments. Works collaboratively with account management, demonstrates an ability to infuse customer-specific business knowledge in the development of project and customer presentations, resulting in delivery of more relevant and credible content.
- Precise and deliberate in communication of difficult or complex ideas. Style of communication reflects thoughtfulness and consideration of a receiver's perspective.
- Proven ability to work cross-functionally with account management personnel in development and execution of projects (models, studies) and presentations designed to highlight the clinical and economic benefit of _____ products.
- Experienced in working collaboratively with investigators in the conceptualization and design of project protocols, as well as ongoing project monitoring and management.
- Demonstrated ability to sell ideas and acquire necessary resources when those ideas evolve into fundable project opportunities. Effective selling of ideas is highly dependent on the ability to secure consensus or buy-in in cross-functional team environments.
- Quality improvement focus. Developed standardized submission and review processes designed to enhance the consistency, efficiency, and quality of the project review process. Responsible for the formation and administration of the project review committee (PRC), which provided internal review for projects submitted by field personnel as well as in-house scientists.
- Proven ability to work effectively in team environments. Able to support conceptualization and development of

economic models and benefits of key products, providing improved access in managed care environments.

* Proven ability to effectively manage up, down, and laterally, across solid as well as dotted line relationships.
* Proven track record working with large customers/accounts in the execution of projects and presentations.
Examples: _____.
* Adaptability. Able to change direction and make necessary adjustments on short notice to meet the needs of the customer (internal and/or internal). Always prepared to move to Plan B.
* Experience. Combination of academic training, years of experience in diverse health care settings, and most recently, superior performance in the support of _____ health outcomes research program. This combined experience will ultimately deliver value to _____ and their customers, as it has for _____.

Imagine the positive impression you would make in any interview with a well thought-out past, present, and future look at you as a resource.

Imagine the conclusion your new boss would make. Imagine also how it would separate you from the others.

As for the 90-day plan, once you have the job, you know precisely what to do for the first three months: Talk about how you will learn the job, the people, and the culture; how you will align goals with your new boss and your new team; and how you will interview, consult, and research. Don't get too detailed. Generalities will help the interviewer dream of you in the job!

REFERENCES

Some of these books and websites have influenced our thinking. Some are for your exploration to see how they will influence you.

Books

Adler, A. (1959). *What Life Should Mean To You*. New York: G. P. Putnam.

Allan, D. (2001). *Getting things done*. New York: Penguin Books.
A fast read and worth it!

Carnegie, D. (1990). *How to win friends and influence people*. New York: Pocket Books.
A great favorite. A classic, and it was written before any of us were born!

Ellis, K. (1998). *The magic lamp: Goal setting for people who hate setting goals*. New York: Three Rivers Press.
Kevin's favorite new/old book!

Ferriss, T. (2007). *The 4-hour work week*. New York: Crown Archetype.
A modern classic, especially if you work with younger colleagues.

Lakein, A. (1989). *How to get control of your time and your life.* New York: Signet.
The classic original: short, direct, easy-to-implement.

Maxey, C. & Bremer, J. (2003). *It's your move: Dealing yourself the best cards in life and work.* Upper Saddle River, NJ: FT/Prentice Hall.
The first Maxey book on balance and your life at work and home.

Maxey, C. & O'Connor, K. (2006). *Present like a pro: A field guide to mastering the art of business, professional, and public speaking.* New York: St. Martin's Press.
Based on our work with physician presenters, scientists, and executives. A beyond-the-basics approach to making a connection with your audience for a lasting memory.

Maxey, C. & O'Connor, K. (2008). *Speak up: A woman's guide to presenting like a pro.* New York: St. Martin's Press.
Requested by our female editor who felt women are judged differently when they speak than are men. We interviewed executive women, and this is the result!

McKenna, P. J. & Maister, D. H. (2002). *First among equals.* New York: The Free Press.
We first found this on an executive client's desk. He managed more than 90 high-level scientists. So we read it. It applies to all professionals regardless of their academic training.

McLuhan, M. (2003). *Understanding media: The extensions of man.* Berkeley, CA: Gingko Press.
Time to review the master now.

Owen, H. (2008). *Open space technology.* San Francisco: Berrett-Koehler.
A terrific tool to engage others in a decision-making process that invites everyone's participation. Can be used in any setting.

Rodenberg, P. (1992). *The right to speak.* New York: Routledge, Inc.
A very special book of wisdom.

Thaler, L. & Koval, R. (2006). *The power of nice*. New York: Currency Doubleday.
Don't let the title fool you!

Tolle, E. (1999). *The power of now*. Novato, CA: New World Library.
A fine book that shouts "perspective"!

Ury, W. (1993). *Getting past no: Negotiating your way from confrontation to cooperation*. New York: Bantam Books.
This is a classic text. Imagine the energy you'd save with a little more cooperation in your life!

Winters, R. (2004). *The green desert: A silent retreat*. New York: Crossroad.
A very good book by a Chicago author. Very much worth the read.

Websites

www.mygoals.com
The title says it all!

www.theworldcafe.com
A simple and profound technique to help others engage with each other and with you.

www.nidoqubein.com
Our colleague and mentor, who sowed the seeds of this book.

I N D E X

A B O U T   T H E   A U T H O R S

Cyndi Maxey, CSP (MA, Northwestern University)

Cyndi Maxey has been an ASTD member since 1982 and a seven-time presenter at the ASTD International Conference. A professional speaker, she holds the Certified Speaking Professional designation—the National Speakers Association's highest earned credential, held by fewer than 200 women internationally. She has owned Maxey Creative Inc. since 1989, specializing in communication that drives profitable performance.

She has published extensively with ASTD in the past, many of her articles have been published in *T + D* magazine, and she co-authored a 2007 ASTD *Infoline* on life and time management with Kevin E. O'Connor, as well as the ASTD Press book, *Training from the Heart: Developing Your Natural Abilities to Inspire the Learner and Drive Performance on the Job* (2000), with co-author Barry Lyerly.

Cyndi also co-authored *It's Your Move: Dealing Yourself the Best Cards in Life and Work* (FT/Prentice-Hall, 2003) with Jill Bremer and *Present Like a Pro: The Field Guide to Mastering the Art of Business, Professional, and Public Speaking* (St. Martin's Press, 2006) and *Speak Up! A Woman's Guide to Presenting Like a Pro* (St. Martin's Press/NYC, 2008) with Kevin E. O'Connor.

Cyndi addresses groups throughout the country on the topics of presentations, training, teambuilding, communication, and leadership. Her active collegiate children and Labrador retriever, Max Maxey, add both chaos and balance to the times of her life.

Contact Cyndi at cmaxey@cyndimaxey.com. You can also visit her website and blog at www.cyndimaxey.com and www.cyndimaxey/blog.com.

Kevin E. O'Connor, CSP (MA, St. Xavier College; MA, Adler School of Professional Psychology; MPS, Loyola University)

Kevin E. O'Connor is a consultant, professional speaker, and author who works with medical and health care professionals who have been promoted to lead teams of their fellow professionals. He facilitates programs on communication, leadership, and creativity, especially in the medical and pharmaceutical fields and in other technical areas.

Kevin is the co-author with Cyndi Maxey of *Present Like a Pro: A Field Guide to Mastering the Art of Business, Professional, and Public Speaking* (St. Martin's Press) and *Speak Up: A Woman's Guide to Presenting Like a Pro*, also published by St. Martin's. He is currently working on a book devoted to finding influence with colleagues who do not directly report to you.

Kevin teaches graduate and undergraduate students at Loyola University of Chicago and at Columbia College, the largest performing arts school in the country. Kevin is a faculty member for the American College of Physician Executives and for the American College of Healthcare Executives and is a consultant for the Accreditation Council for Pharmaceutical Education.

Kevin is a CSP (Certified Speaking Professional). Less than 570 persons in the world hold this honor for speaking excellence. He has three master's degrees and is the author and co-author of seven books.

Kevin works extensively with schools and organizations for those who are blind and visually impaired and lives in the northwest suburbs of Chicago with his wife and his son's retired Guide Dog for the Blind, Phoenix.

Contact Kevin at kevin@kevinoc.com. You can also visit his website at www.kevinoc.com.

THE ASTD MISSION:

Through exceptional learning and performance, we create a world that works better.

The American Society for Training & Development provides world-class professional development opportunities, content, networking, and resources for workplace learning and performance professionals.

Dedicated to helping members increase their relevance, enhance their skills, and align learning to business results, ASTD sets the standard for best practices within the profession.

The society is recognized for shaping global discussions on workforce development and providing the tools to demonstrate the impact of learning on the organizational bottom line. ASTD represents the profession's interests to corporate executives, policy makers, academic leaders, small business owners, and consultants through world-class content, convening opportunities, professional development, and awards and recognition.

Resources
- *T+D (Training + Development)* Magazine
- ASTD Press
- Industry Newsletters
- Research and Benchmarking
- Representation to Policy Makers

Professional Development
- Certificate Programs
- Conferences and Workshops
- Online Learning
- CPLP™ Certification Through the ASTD Certification Institute
- Career Center and Job Bank

Networking
- Local Chapters
- Online Communities
- ASTD Connect
- Benchmarking Forum
- Learning Executives Network

Awards and Best Practices
- ASTD BEST Awards
- Excellence in Practice Awards
- E-Learning Courseware Certification (ECC) Through the ASTD Certification Institute

Learn more about ASTD at www.astd.org.
1.800.628.2783 (U.S.) or 1.703.683.8100
customercare@astd.org